STECK-VAUGHN

TABE® Reading

Fundamentals

Focus on Skills

LEVEL E

STECK-VAUGHN

TABE® Reading

Fundamentals

Focus on Skills

LEVEL E

Steck Vaughn®

HOUGHTON MIFFLIN HARCOURT

www.SteckVaughn.com/AdultEd
800-289-4490

Reviewer

Gail Johnson Price
ABE/GED Instructor
Americana Learning Center
Jefferson County Public Schools—Adult Education
Louisville, Kentucky

Contents

To the Learner vi

To the Instructor 3

Steck-Vaughn's *TABE Fundamentals* Program at a Glance 5

TABE Objective Interpret Graphic Information
Lesson 1 Signs 6
Lesson 2 Maps 8
Lesson 3 Graphs 10
Lesson 4 Consumer Materials 12
Lesson 5 Forms 14
Lesson 6 Dictionary Usage 16
TABE Review: Interpret Graphic Information 18

TABE Objective Words in Context
Lesson 7 Same Meaning 22
Lesson 8 Opposite Meaning 24
Lesson 9 Appropriate Word 26
TABE Review: Words in Context 28

TABE Objective Recall Information
Lesson 10 Details 31
Lesson 11 Sequence 33
Lesson 12 Stated Concepts 35
TABE Review: Recall Information 37

TABE Objective Construct Meaning
Lesson 13 Character Aspects 40
Lesson 14 Main Idea 42
Lesson 15 Cause/Effect 44
Lesson 16 Compare/Contrast 46
Lesson 17 Conclusions 48
TABE Review: Construct Meaning 50

TABE Objective Evaluate/Extend Meaning
Lesson 18 Fact/Opinion 54
Lesson 19 Predict Outcomes 56
TABE Review: Evaluate/Extend Meaning 58

Performance Assessment: Reading 63

Answers and Explanations 77

Answer Sheet . . . . inside back cover

To the Learner

You are taking an important step in your educational career by studying for the TABE. This book will help you do your best on the TABE. You'll also find hints and strategies that will help you prepare for test day. Practice these skills—your success lies in your hands.

What Is the TABE?

TABE stands for the Tests of Adult Basic Education. These paper-and-pencil tests, published by McGraw-Hill, measure your progress on basic skills. The tests get harder with each level because you continue to be tested on skills learned at earlier levels. There are seven tests in all: Reading, Mathematics Computation, Applied Mathematics, Language, Vocabulary, Language Mechanics, and Spelling.

TABE Levels E, M, D, and A

Test	Number of Items	Suggested Working Time (in minutes)
1 Reading	50	50
2 Mathematics Computation	40	24
3 Applied Mathematics	50	50
4 Language	55	55
5 Vocabulary	20	14
6 Language Mechanics	20	14
7 Spelling	20	10

Test 1 Reading

This test measures basic reading skills. The main concepts covered by this test are word meaning, critical thinking, and understanding basic information.

Test 2 Mathematics Computation

This test covers adding, subtracting, multiplying, and dividing. On this test, you must use these skills with whole numbers and decimals.

Test 3 Applied Mathematics

This test links mathematical ideas to real-world situations. Skills you do every day, such as budgeting, cooking, and doing your taxes, all require math. This test covers pre-algebra, algebra, and geometry.

Test 4 Language

This test requires you to analyze different types of writing, such as business letters, job reports, and essays. For each task, you have to show you understand good writing skills.

Test 5 Vocabulary

This test measures how well you can identify the meanings of words. You must also find words that mean the same or the opposite of some words. This test also measures whether you can find the meaning of a word with the help of other words in the same sentence or paragraph.

Test 6 Language Mechanics

This test measures how much you know about the elements that make a good sentence, such as capitalization and punctuation. You must also find the most important sentence, called the topic sentence, in a paragraph.

Test 7 Spelling

This test measures your ability to spell correctly. The spelling words on this test are words that many people misspell and words that are commonly used in adult writing.

Test-Taking Tips

1. Read the directions very carefully. Make sure you read them word for word. If you are not sure what the directions mean, ask the person giving the test to explain them to you.

2. Read each question carefully. Know what the question means and what you have to do.

3. Read all of the answers carefully, even if you think you know the answer.

4. Make sure that the passage supports your answer. Don't answer without checking the passage. Don't rely on outside knowledge alone.

5. Answer all of the questions.

6. Erase any extra marks before you finish.

7. Don't change an answer unless you are sure your first answer is wrong.

8. If you get nervous, stop for a while. Take a few breaths and relax.

How to Use *TABE Fundamentals*

Step-by-Step Instruction In Levels E, M, and D, each lesson starts with the step-by-step instruction of a skill. This instruction is followed by practice items. Check your work in the Answers and Explanations section in the back of the book. The Level A books only contain practice for each skill covered on the TABE. They do not include step-by-step instructions.

Reviews The lessons in Levels E, M, and D are grouped by TABE Objectives. At the end of each TABE Objective, there is a Review. Complete each Review before continuing to work.

Performance Assessment At the end of every book, there is a special section called Performance Assessment. This section will help you understand the actual TABE.

Answer Sheet In each book, there is a practice bubble-in answer sheet. Fill in the answer sheet carefully. For each item, mark only one numbered space on the answer sheet. Mark the space beside the number that matches the item.

Strategies and Hints Pay careful attention to the TABE Strategies and Hints throughout the books. TABE Strategies are test-taking tips. Hints give you extra information.

Setting Goals

Below is a form that will help you set your goals.

Section 1. Why do you want to do well on the TABE? Take some time now to set your short-term and long-term goals.

Section 2. Making a schedule is one way to set priorities. Deadlines will help you stay focused.

Section 3. Your goals may change over time. These changes are natural. Checking your progress on a regular basis helps you reach your goals.

1. Your Goals

What is your long-term goal for using this book?

_____

_____

Identify the short-term goals or the smaller steps you need to take to reach your long-term goal.

Content area	What I Know	What I Want to Learn
Reading	_____	_____
Language	_____	_____
Math	_____	_____
Other	_____	_____

2. Make a Schedule

Set some deadlines for the short-term goals you named in Section 1.

Short-Term Goals	Begin Date	End Date
_____	_____	_____
_____	_____	_____

3. Celebrate Your Success

Note the progress you've made. If you made changes in your goals, record them here, too.

_____

_____

To the Instructor

About TABE

The seven Tests of Adult Basic Education in Reading, Mathematics Computation, Applied Mathematics, Language, Vocabulary, Language Mechanics, and Spelling are designed to meet the needs of adult learners in TABE programs. Written and designed to be relevant to adult learners' lives and interests, this material focuses on the problem-solving skills that are typical of adult needs. Because of the increasing importance of thinking skills in any curriculum, *TABE Fundamentals* focuses on critical thinking throughout the material presented for each TABE Objective.

Uses of the TABE

Instructional

From an instructional point of view, the TABE allows instructors to assess learners' entry level skills as they begin adult programs. The TABE also allows instructors to diagnose learners' strengths and weaknesses in order to determine appropriate areas on which to focus instruction. Finally, the TABE allows instructors and institutions to monitor learners' progress.

Administrative

The TABE allows institutions to assess classes in general and measure the effectiveness of instruction and whether learners are making progress.

Governmental

The TABE provides a means of assessing a school or program's effectiveness.

The National Reporting System (NRS) and the TABE

Adult education and literacy programs are federally funded and thus accountable to the federal government. The National Reporting System monitors adult education. Developed with the help of adult educators, the NRS sets the reporting requirements for adult education programs around the country. The information collected by the NRS is used to assess the effectiveness of adult education programs and make necessary improvements.

According to the NRS guidelines, states select the method of assessment appropriate for their needs. States can assess educational gain either through standardized tests or through performance-based assessment. Among the standardized tests typically used under NRS guidelines is the TABE, which meets the NRS standards both for administrative procedures and for scoring.

The three main methods used by the NRS to collect data are:

1. **Direct program reporting,** which occurs from the moment of enrollment
2. **Local follow-up surveys,** which involve learners' employment or academic goals
3. **Data matching,** or sharing data among agencies serving the same clients, so that outcomes unique to each program can be identified

A key measure defined by the NRS is educational gain, which is an assessment of the improvements in learners' reading, writing, speaking, listening, and other skills during their instruction. Programs assess educational gain at every stage of instruction.

NRS Functioning Level	Grade Level TABE	TABE 9/10 Scale Scores
Beginning ABE Literacy	0–1.9	Reading........................ 367 and below Total Math.................... 313 and below Language .... 389 and below
Beginning Basic Education	2–3.9	Reading........................ 368–460 Total Math.................... 314–441 Language 390–490
Low Intermediate Basic Education	4–5.9	Reading........................ 461–517 Total Math.................... 442–505 Language 491–523
High Intermediate Basic Education	6–8.9	Reading........................ 518–566 Total Math.................... 506–565 Language 524–559
Low Adult Secondary Education	9–10.9	Reading........................ 567–595 Total Math.................... 566–594 Language 560–585

Two of the major goals of the NRS are academic achievement and workplace readiness. Educational gain is a means to reach these goals. As learners move through the adult education curriculum, the progress they make should help them either obtain or keep employment or obtain a diploma, whether at the secondary school level or higher. The TABE is flexible enough to meet both the academic and workplace goals set forth by the NRS.

Using *TABE Fundamentals*

Adult Basic Education Placement
From the outset, the TABE allows effective placement of learners. You can use the *TABE Fundamentals* series to support instruction of those skills that need development.

High School Equivalency
Placement often involves predicting learners' success on the GED® Tests. Each level of *TABE Fundamentals* covers Reading, Language, Spelling, Vocabulary, Language Mechanics, and Applied and Computational Math to allow learners to focus their attention where it is needed.

Assessing Progress
Each TABE skill is covered in a lesson. These lessons are grouped by TABE Objectives. At the end of each TABE Objective, there is a Review. Use these Reviews to determine if the learners need to review any of the skills before continuing to work.

At the end of the book, there is a special section called Performance Assessment. This section is similar to the TABE test. It has the same number and types of items. You can use the Performance Assessment as a timed pretest or post-test with your learners or as a more general review for the actual TABE test.

Steck-Vaughn's *TABE Fundamentals* Program at a Glance
The chart on the following page provides a quick overview of the elements of Steck-Vaughn's *TABE Fundamentals* series. Use this chart to match the TABE objectives with the skill areas for each level. This chart will prove useful whenever you need to determine which objectives match the specific skill areas you need to cover.

TABE OBJECTIVE

	Level E		Level M		Level D		Level A
	Reading	Language	Reading	Language and Spelling	Reading	Language and Spelling	Reading, Language, and Spelling
Reading							
Interpret Graphic Information	✦		✦		✦		✦
Words in Context	✦		✦		✦		✦
Recall Information	✦		✦		✦		✦
Construct Meaning	✦		✦		✦		✦
Evaluate/Extend Meaning	✦		✦		✦		✦
Language and Mechanics							
Usage		✦		✦		✦	✦
Sentence Formation		✦		✦		✦	✦
Paragraph Development		✦		✦		✦	✦
Capitalization		✦		✦		✦	✦
Punctuation		✦		✦		✦	✦
Writing Conventions		✦		✦		✦	✦
Vocabulary							
Word Meaning		✦					
Multimeaning Words		✦					
Words in Context		✦					
Spelling							
Vowels		✦		✦		✦	✦
Consonants		✦		✦		✦	✦
Structural Unit		✦		✦		✦	✦

	Level E	Level M		Level D		Level A
	Mathematics	Math Computation	Applied Math	Math Computation	Applied Math	Computational and Applied Math
Mathematics Computation						
Addition of Whole Numbers	✦	✦				
Subtraction of Whole Numbers	✦	✦				
Multiplication of Whole Numbers	✦			✦		
Division of Whole Numbers	✦			✦		
Decimals	✦	✦		✦		✦
Fractions		✦		✦		✦
Integers		✦		✦		✦
Percents				✦		✦
Order of Operation				✦		✦
Applied Mathematics						
Numbers and Number Operations	✦		✦		✦	✦
Computation in Context	✦		✦		✦	✦
Estimation	✦		✦		✦	✦
Measurement	✦		✦		✦	✦
Geometry and Spatial Sense	✦		✦		✦	✦
Data Analysis	✦		✦		✦	✦
Statistics and Probability	✦		✦		✦	✦
Patterns, Functions, Algebra	✦		✦		✦	✦
Problem Solving and Reasoning	✦		✦		✦	✦

Lesson 1 Signs

Signs are everywhere. They give you information. They warn you of danger. They help you find your way. They tell you about things you may want to buy. You may see hundreds of signs each week.

The TABE will ask you questions about signs. Read all of the words on a sign to find out what you need to know.

Example **Read the sign. What kind of information does this sign give?**

_____

On one day of the week, the business is not open at all.

Which day is that? _____

BUSINESS HOURS

Monday - Thursday	8:00 AM — 6:00 PM
Friday	8:00 AM — 9:00 PM
Saturday	7:00 AM — 8:00 PM
Sunday	CLOSED

The sign gives information by showing the hours that a business is open. Note that the business does not keep the same hours every day. You can see from the sign that the store is not open at all on Sundays.

Test Example

Read the sign above. Then do Number 1.

1 On which day is this business open latest?

   A Monday   C Friday

   B Tuesday   D Saturday

TABE Strategy

Circle or underline important words in the question, like *latest*.

1 C The business is open until 9 o'clock on Friday nights. On Mondays and Tuesdays (options A and B), the business closes at 6:00. On Saturdays (option D), the business closes at 8:00.

Read the sign that shows where offices are in a building. Then do Numbers 1 through 3.

The Carlson Building Directory

American Insurance	120
Barnes Law Offices	200
C and L Computer Repair	114
Hall Eyewear	124
Lientz, Ray, Tax Preparation	214
Nelson, Dr. Maria	128
Smith Travel Agency	320
Wallace Watch Repair	308

1 How is this building directory arranged?

A by office numbers

B by floors

C by alphabetical order

D by types of businesses

2 What office number would you go to for new eye glasses?

F 200

G 124

H 320

J 308

3 Which office belongs to Dr. Nelson?

A 114

B 128

C 214

D 320

You are in a large store that sells things for the home. Read the signs. Then do Numbers 4 and 5.

Lawn & Garden	Paint & Wallpaper	Door Hardware	Kitchen Appliances

4 In what aisle would you be most likely to find paintbrushes?

F Lawn & Garden

G Paint & Wallpaper

H Door Hardware

J Kitchen Appliances

5 What aisle is most likely to have a door handle?

A Lawn & Garden

B Paint & Wallpaper

C Door Hardware

D Kitchen Appliances

Check your answers on page 77.

Lesson 2 — Maps

The TABE will ask you questions about maps. A map gives readers a picture of a place. A map shows where places can be found in a certain area. Maps can show very large areas, such as a map of the United States. A map can also show cities, towns, roads, bodies of water, and other details about a place.

Maps can also give big pictures of very small areas. These maps often show a lot of details about the areas. The places shown on a map are in the same position as they are in real life.

Example Look at this map. How many baseball fields are there in Sweeny Baseball
Complex? _____

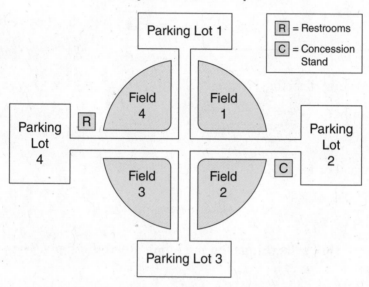

This map shows four fields in the complex.

Test Example

Study the map above. Then do Number 1.

1 What parking lot should you park in if you have a game on
   Field 4 and you need to use the restroom?

   A Parking Lot 1   C Parking Lot 3

   B Parking Lot 2   D Parking Lot 4

1 **D** Parking Lot 4 is the closest lot to both Field 4 and the
       restrooms. Parking Lot 1 (option A) is close to Field 4 but
       not to the restrooms. Parking Lots 2 (option B) and 3
       (option C) are not close to Field 4 or the restrooms.

Study this map of a park. Then do Numbers 1 through 4.

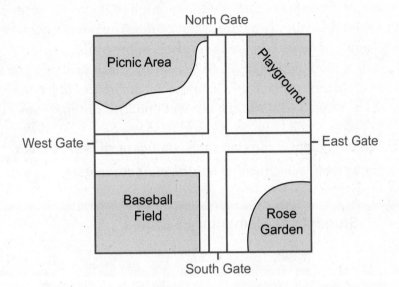

1. If you enter the park through the South Gate, what will you see on your left?

   A picnic area

   B rose garden

   C baseball field

   D playground

2. If you enter the park through the North Gate, you'll walk between what two areas?

   F picnic area and baseball field

   G rose garden and playground

   H baseball field and rose garden

   J picnic area and playground

3. If you enter the park through the West Gate, you'll walk between what two areas?

   A baseball field and rose garden

   B rose garden and playground

   C playground and picnic area

   D picnic area and baseball field

4. The rose garden is between which two gates?

   F East and South

   G South and West

   H West and North

   J North and East

Check your answers on page 77.

Lesson 3 Graphs

A graph is a picture of information. Some graphs use bars to show facts, numbers, or other information. By showing differences in information, graphs help you to compare the information.

A **bar graph** shows information with bars or thick lines. The bars may move up and down or side to side. A bar's length matches a value or number on the graph.

To understand a graph, read the title and labels carefully. Make sure that you understand what the graph is showing. Then look at the bars. Compare the differences in lengths. Move your finger from the end of each bar straight across to the number line. This number shows the value of the bar.

Example Look at this bar graph. It compares the number of students in four elementary schools. Which school has the most students? _____

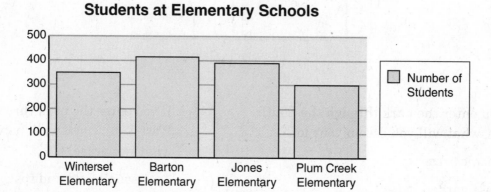

Students at Elementary Schools

Look at all the bars. Which is the tallest? The bar for Barton Elementary is higher than the others. This means that this school has more students than the other schools. Draw a line from the top of this bar to the number on the left. This number shows how many students go to Barton Elementary School: more than 400.

Test Example

Study the bar graph above. Then do Number 1.

1 How many students attend Plum Creek Elementary School?

    A 250　　　　　　　　C 350

    B 300　　　　　　　　D 400

> **1 B** The top of the bar for Plum Creek Elementary touches the line labeled 300. Option A (250) is not correct because the bar for Plum Creek goes higher than this value. Options C (350) and D (400) are not correct because the bar for Plum Creek does not reach these values.

Study the bar graph. Then do Numbers 1 through 4.

Shipping Company Employees

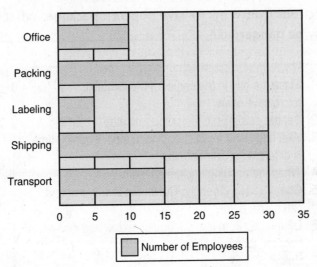

Number of Employees

1 What information does the graph provide about the shipping company?

   A how many trucks it owns

   B how much money it made last year

   C how many employees it has

   D how many people applied for jobs last year

2 How many employees work in the office?

   F 5

   G 10

   H 20

   J 30

3 What two groups have the same number of employees?

   A office and packing

   B packing and transport

   C labeling and shipping

   D shipping and transport

4 Which group has the most employees?

   F shipping

   G labeling

   H transport

   J office

Check your answers on page 77.

Lesson 4 Consumer Materials

When you buy and use a product, you are a consumer. Products that you buy often come with written information. This information helps you understand how to use the products.

Example Read these directions from a microwave popcorn package. What part of this process may be dangerous? _____

> **THIS SIDE UP**   **THIS SIDE UP**
>
> 1. Place the bag in the center of the turntable in a microwave oven.
> 2. Set the power on high for four minutes.
> 3. Wait and listen for the popping to stop. Popping time is different for different ovens.
> 4. When the popping ends, stop the oven.
> 5. Open the bag carefully. The steam is very hot and can cause burns.
> 6. Lift the bag from the top, and open the bag away from the face and body.
> 7. Enjoy!

Consumer or buyer directions often have safety warnings. Here, in steps 5 and 6, you read warnings to be careful while opening the bag; the steam from the bag can cause burns.

Test Example

Read the directions from the popcorn package above.
Then do Number 1.

1 Why should you wait and listen after turning on the microwave oven?

   A The bag should stay in the center of the oven.

   B You must make sure the turntable turns.

   C The oven may not stop by itself.

   D Different ovens may have different popping times.

1 D You must wait and listen for the popping to stop. As noted in step 3, the popping time depends on each different oven. Option A is discussed before step 3. Options B and C are not mentioned in the directions.

Read the warning label for a cleaning product. Then do Numbers 1 through 5.

> **WARNING:**
> Keep out of reach of children.
> Harmful or fatal if swallowed.
> May burn eyes and skin.
>
> **FIRST AID:**
> In case of skin or eye contact, flush with cold water for 15 minutes. If swallowed, rinse mouth with cool water. Drink a large glass of water or milk. Get immediate help from a doctor or poison control center at 800-555-5555.

1 What information does the FIRST AID section give you?

A how to use the product

B fire safety tips

C where to call for help

D what the product is made of

2 Why should the cleaner be kept away from children?

F The bottle is too hard to open.

G The product can be dangerous.

H Children can't read.

J Cleaners have bad smells.

3 In case of skin or eye contact, how long should you flush with cold water?

A 15 minutes

B 1 minute

C 800 minutes

D 15 seconds

4 Who should you call if someone drinks some of this product?

F a doctor

G a lawyer

H the police

J the fire department

5 This label tells you that the product is

A safe for everyone

B only safe if you wear a mask

C dangerous if swallowed

D dangerous for animals

Check your answers on page 77.

Lesson 5 · Forms

A form is a kind of document that has blank spaces where you must fill in information. Knowing how to read and fill out forms correctly is a skill that will help you apply for jobs, get loans, and enroll in school.

Example   **Study this form. What is the purpose of the form?** _____

Newsmouth Magazine

Get a one-year subscription of Newsmouth Magazine at a special rate. A full year of Newsmouth is only $48. That's less than one dollar per issue. Subscribe today!

Please print the following information. Then return the card.

Name _____

Street _____

City _____ State _____ Zip Code _____

Choose one of the following:

☐ One year at $48

☐ **Extra Savings!** Get two years for $90!

This form will help you order a magazine. You fill out your name and address. Then you return the form to the magazine. In return, you will receive copies of the magazine. Read the entire form before you begin to fill it out. This will help you understand what information is needed. When you are sure of the information, write it in the blank spaces. Sometimes forms ask for other information. For example, you may need to make a decision or choice about something.

Test Example

Read the magazine order form above. Then do Number 1.

1 What choice does this form ask you to make?

   A whether you will pay now or get a bill

   C whether you want to get the magazine daily or weekly

   B whether you want to get the magazine for one year or two years

   D whether you will take the magazine

1 B The form asks you to choose between a one- or two-year subscription by checking a box. Option A is incorrect because the form says nothing about the type of payment. Option C is incorrect because the form says nothing about a daily or weekly subscription. Option D is incorrect because the form does not ask whether you will subscribe.

This rebate form is used to get money back after a purchase of Zoom Motor Oil. Read the form.
Then do Numbers 1 through 4.

$1 Cash Back Rebate Form

Thank you for buying Zoom Motor Oil. This rebate form gets you $1 per
quart cash back on the purchase of Zoom Motor Oil. The limit on this
rebate offer is eight (8) quarts (or $8). Your purchase must be made
between November 1, 2009 and January 31, 2010.

Please print the following information.

Name _____

Street _____

City _____ State _____ Zip _____

Number of quarts purchased _____ Date of purchase _____

Name of store where purchased _____

To get your rebate, follow these steps:
1) Make a copy of your sales receipt and keep it for your records.
2) Complete this rebate form.
3) Mail this rebate form and the original receipt to the following address:

     Zoom Motor Oil, Inc.
     Rebate Offer
     6422 Willis Drive
     Santa Clara, CA 95054

1 What is the purpose of this form?

  A get cash back on the purchase of oil

  B order oil by the case from Zoom

  C return unneeded quarts of oil

  D get a free extra quart of oil

2 What is the limit on this offer?

  F 1 quart

  G 4 quarts

  H 8 quarts

  J no limit

3 What is the last date of purchase that
still qualifies for this rebate?

  A November 1, 2009

  B November 1, 2010

  C January 31, 2009

  D January 31, 2010

4 Other than the form, what information is
needed to get the rebate?

  F the label from a quart of Zoom Oil

  G a copy of a canceled check

  H an original sales receipt for Zoom Oil

  J the bar code from the Zoom oil

Check your answers on page 77.

Lesson 6 Dictionary Usage

A dictionary entry lists a word. The entry shows how to say the word, or pronounce it. The next part shows the part of speech of the word. Words can be nouns, verbs, adjectives, or other parts of speech. Then the meanings of the word are listed. Sometimes the entry includes examples, as well.

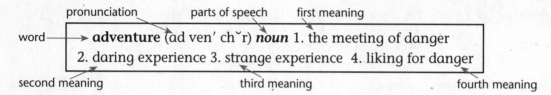

You can see that *adventure* is a noun that has four meanings. Note that two of the meanings have something to do with danger.

Example **Which meaning of *adventure* might be used to describe an encounter with a wild bear?** _____

Wild bears are dangerous. You would be using the first definition of *adventure*, "the meeting of danger," if you used the word to describe a meeting with a wild bear. This meaning is more appropriate than "daring" or "strange," and you don't have to like danger to encounter a bear in the wild!

Test Example

Read the dictionary entry above. Then do Number 1.

1 "The mountain climber has a real sense of adventure." Which definition of the word *adventure* is used in this sentence?

   A definition 1

   B definition 2

   C definition 3

   D definition 4

> **1 D** It is likely that someone who enjoys climbing mountains has a liking for danger. Options A, B, and C do not fit because the sentence tells about a character trait rather than an actual experience.

Read the dictionary entry for the word *benefit*. Then do Numbers 1 through 3.

---

benefit (ben′ ə fĭt) *noun* **1.** something that makes life better **2.** payments made by an insurance company, public agency, or the like **3.** any event that gives money to help a certain person, group, or cause **4.** something that gives an advantage

---

1 "What kinds of benefits does your insurance offer?" Which definition of the word *benefits* is used in this sentence?

  A definition 1

  B definition 2

  C definition 3

  D definition 4

2 "You will benefit from good eating habits." Which definition of the word *benefit* is used in this sentence?

  F definition 1

  G definition 2

  H definition 3

  J definition 4

3 "I organized a benefit that would give money to people in need." Which definition of the word *benefit* is used in this sentence?

  A definition 1

  B definition 2

  C definition 3

  D definition 4

Read the dictionary entry for the word *free*. Then do Numbers 4 and 5.

---

free (ˈfrē) *adjective* **1.** not controlled or limited; able to do what one wants **2.** no longer a prisoner or slave **3.** not affected by something unpleasant **4.** not busy

---

4 "The city should be free from pollution by 2014." Which definition of the word *free* is used in this sentence?

  F definition 1

  G definition 2

  H definition 3

  J definition 4

5 "I am busy this morning, but I'm free this afternoon." Which definition of the word *free* is used in this sentence?

  A definition 1

  B definition 2

  C definition 3

  D definition 4

Check your answers on page 78.

This is a sign from a department store. Read the sign. Then do Numbers 1 and 2.

SALE°

SPRING TAG SALE!

Take **$5 off** the price of any shoe marked with a red tag!
Take **$10 off** the price of any shoe marked with a yellow tag!

Sale starts Wednesday at 8:00 AM and ends Sunday at closing!

1 What items are on sale in the department store?

  A purses
  B jewelry
  C men's wear
  D shoes

2 Which items are $5 off?

  F items with yellow tags
  G items with red tags
  H items with red or yellow tags
  J all items

Read the dictionary entry for the word *run*. Then do Numbers 3 and 4.

> **run** (ʻrən) *verb* **1.** to move quickly, so that both feet leave the ground between each step **2.** to be in charge of the day-to-day operations of an organization **3.** to be a candidate in a race or election **4.** to function or operate

3 "Mr. Sandoval has what it takes to run our company." Which definition of the word *run* is used in this sentence?

  A definition 1
  B definition 2
  C definition 3
  D definition 4

4 "I've decided to run for treasurer of our neighborhood association." Which definition of the word *run* is used in this sentence?

  F definition 1
  G definition 2
  H definition 3
  J definition 4

This bar graph shows the number of tornadoes in four states. Read the bar graph. Then do Numbers 5 through 8.

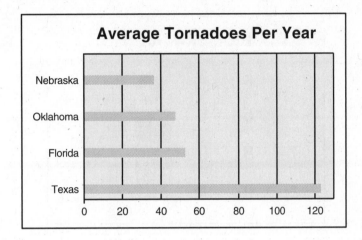

Average Tornadoes Per Year

5 Of these four states, which state has the most tornadoes?

   A Nebraska

   B Oklahoma

   C Florida

   D Texas

6 Which state has the fewest tornadoes?

   F Nebraska

   G Oklahoma

   H Florida

   J Texas

7 This graph shows that Oklahoma has about how many tornadoes per year?

   A 26

   B 47

   C 61

   D 88

8 Based on the information in this graph, which of the following statements is true?

   F Oklahoma has more tornadoes than Florida.

   G Texas has more than twice as many tornadoes as any other state.

   H Nebraska has fewer than 20 tornadoes per year.

   J Florida has about a hundred tornadoes per year.

This hotel phone gives you information on whom to call if you need help. Review the information on the phone. Then do Numbers 9 and 10.

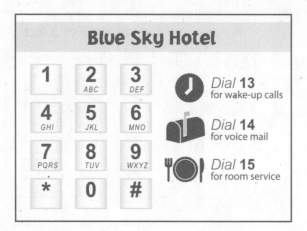

9 What number would you call if you wanted the hotel operator to call you in the morning to wake you up?

A 12

B 13

C 14

D 15

10 What number would you call if you needed to get your voice mail messages?

F 12

G 13

H 14

J 15

Study this sign-in form used at a doctor's office. Then do Numbers 11 and 12.

White Oak Dentists—Drs. Orvilla and Cooke		
*Please expect to wait approximately 15 minutes.		
Name	Appointment Time*	Check-in Time*
1.		
2.		

11 What information is requested on the form?

A patient's name

B doctor's name

C insurance information

D dental complaint

12 How long should a patient expect to have to wait in the waiting room?

F It depends on the patient's appointment time.

G It depends on the patient's check-in time.

H about 15 minutes

J about 30 minutes

Study the map. Then do Numbers 13 through 16.

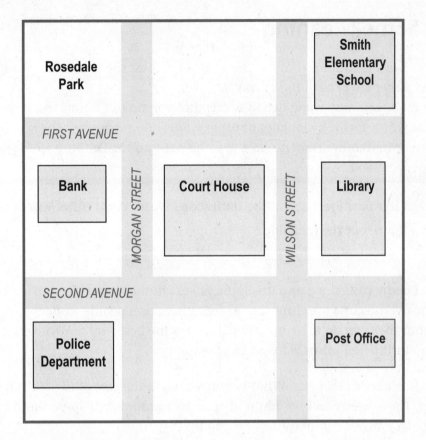

13 What is on the corner of Second Avenue and Morgan Street?

   A library

   B post office

   C school

   D police department

14 What is right across the street from the school?

   F park

   G bank

   H library

   J police department

15 What is the location of Smith Elementary School?

   A First Avenue and Morgan Street

   B Second Avenue and Wilson Street

   C First Avenue and Wilson Street

   D Second Avenue and Morgan Street

16 Which building is the closest to Rosedale Park?

   F post office

   G school

   H bank

   J police department

Check your answers on page 78.

Lesson 7 Same Meaning

Many words have meanings that are the same or almost the same. For example, you might describe a <u>wet</u> paper towel as <u>damp</u> or <u>moist</u>.

When you read, you may come across words that you do not know. You may be able to figure out what these words mean by looking at other words and sentences. These words may be in the same sentence or in another sentence in the same paragraph. The way words are used gives the whole passage a context.

Example **Read this passage. Look at the underlined word. What other words help you figure out the meaning?**

Energy costs are going up. Some prices change very little, but the overall costs are climbing. As fuel prices rise, people wonder what they can do to save money. Perhaps the best way to deal with <u>mounting</u> fuel prices is to use less energy.

This passage is about fuel costs. What is happening to the cost of fuel? It is **going up**. The prices are **climbing**. These words and the main idea of the paragraph help you understand that, in this passage, *mounting* means "climbing" or "going up."

Write another word that has the same meaning as <u>mounting</u>. _____

Test Example

Read the passage about sharing too much information over the Internet. Then do Number 1.

It is tempting to post <u>personal</u> information on the Internet. Message boards, blogs, and popular social networking sites make it easy to share too much information about yourself. But be careful. Criminals can use the Internet to steal your personal information, creating problems and possibly dangerous situations for you and your family.

1 Based on this passage, *personal* means about the same as

A funny   C truthful

B private   D boring

1 B The word *personal* means "private." If a criminal got your private information, he or she could create problems for you. The other options are incorrect because posting funny (option A), truthful (option C), or boring (option D) information would not lead to potentially dangerous situations if a criminal got a hold of it.

Practice

Read this passage about crowded roads. Then do Numbers 1 through 4.

Our streets and highways are becoming more and more <u>clogged</u>. Cars, trucks, and buses block every traffic lane. Rush hour jams can be <u>problematic</u>, especially if they make you late for work or an important appointment. Even when new highways are built, traffic soon fills them completely. The size of the road hardly matters. We need to find new ways to <u>ease</u> the overcrowding of our roads. If we don't, no one is going to get to work on time.

1 The passage says that streets and highways are becoming more and more clogged. *Clogged* means about the same as

A open

B safe

C blocked

D beautiful

2 What word in the second sentence helps you understand the word *clogged*?

F block

G every

H traffic

J lane

3 The passage says that rush hour jams can be problematic. *Problematic* means about the same as

A funny

B dangerous

C easy

D troublesome

4 The passage says that we need to find ways to ease the overcrowding of our roads. *Ease* means about the same as

F record

G lighten

H study

J ignore

Check your answers on page 78.

Lesson 8   Opposite Meanings

Some words can have opposite meanings of other words. For example, *up* means the opposite of *down*, and *hot* is the opposite of *cold*.

Sometimes you can discover the meaning of an unknown word when you know its opposite. For example, you might not know the meaning of the word *timid*. However, it might help to know that *timid* is the opposite of *brave*.

Some passages compare things by using opposites. In this case, you can use information in the surrounding words and sentences to help you understand the meaning of a new word.

Example   **Read this passage. Look at the underlined word. Based on the other words and information in the passage, what do you think the word means?** _____

My favorite baseball players are <u>trustworthy</u>. They don't lie or cheat. They keep their tempers, and they respect their teammates. They also respect the players on other teams. They can be counted on to do their best work.

This writer thinks highly of a certain type of player. You can tell what trustworthy players are by the other words and descriptions in the passage. These players don't lie or cheat. They hold their tempers. They show respect for others and can be counted on to do what is right. This information helps you get a better understanding of the meaning of the word *trustworthy*.

Write a word that has the opposite meaning of *trustworthy*. _____

Test Example

Read the passage about communication. Then do Number 1.

The ways that we stay in touch with people have changed a lot in the last 20 years. These days, speed matters. Today we talk to one another using emails, <u>instant</u> messages, and cell phones. The days of writing, or for that matter slowly reading, a long letter are quickly fading into history.

1   Which of these words means the <u>opposite</u> of *instant* as it is used in this passage?

A   important   C   surprise

B   immediate   D   slow

1 **D** The word *instant* means "quick" or "immediate." Since the question asks for the opposite meaning of *instant*, option D, *slow*, is correct. Options A and C are not related to the meaning of *instant*. Option B means the same thing as *instant*, not the opposite.

Practice

This passage is about one family's 4ᵗʰ of July tradition. Read the passage. Then do Numbers 1 through 4.

My family lives <u>scattered</u> all over the state. While some of us stayed in our hometown, others went away to college, got married, and started their families in other cities. Even though we don't get to see each other very often, we do make it a point to get together at least once a year, on the 4ᵗʰ of July. This summer holiday is the <u>ideal</u> opportunity for a family reunion, and our hometown's location near the beach makes it the perfect destination to escape the summer heat. The <u>thunderous</u> fireworks on the 4ᵗʰ of July create the <u>festive</u> atmosphere that makes our reunion special every year.

1 Which of these words means the <u>opposite</u> of *scattered* as it is used in this passage?

A spread

B gathered

C alone

D stretched

2 Which of these words means the <u>opposite</u> of *ideal* as it is used in this passage?

F perfect

G best

H satisfactory

J awful

3 Which of these words means the <u>opposite</u> of *thunderous* as it is used in this passage?

A quiet

B loud

C booming

D colorful

4 Which of these words means the <u>opposite</u> of *festive* as it is used in this passage?

F celebratory

G serious

H playful

J silly

Check your answers on page 79.

Appropriate Word

When you're reading, you can use the other words and sentences in the passage to give you clues about the subject matter. This is called using context clues. Context clues can help you determine the appropriate, or best fitting, word to use.

Example

Read this passage. What word or phrase would fit best in the blank: *engine*, *radio*, or *air conditioner*? _____

Riley loves music. It always makes her feel better when she's having a bad day. Riley had a rough day at work. She can't wait to get back to her car, turn on her _____, and sing along with some good songs.

Did you pick *radio*? Words and phrases like *music*, *car*, *sing along*, and *good songs* give you clues that *radio* is the best fit for the blank. It doesn't make sense to turn on the engine or air conditioner to sing along with some good songs.

It is important not to overthink questions like these. You might say to yourself, "You have to turn on the engine to get the radio to work so that you can sing along with some good songs." Remember that the right answer is the most obvious answer, not the one you have to twist around to make it fit.

Test Example

Read the sentences. Then do Number 1.

1 It was cold outside. Marisa made sure to grab her _____ before she walked out the door.

   A swimsuit

   B sunglasses

   C purse

   D jacket

1 D The first sentence says that it was "cold outside." A swimsuit (option A), sunglasses (option B), and purse (option C) do not make sense in the context of cold weather.

Read each item. Then do Numbers 1 through 8.

1 I've been so emotional lately. I cry whenever a _____ commercial comes on.

   A happy

   B sad

   C funny

   D scary

2 There have been a lot of layoffs at Carin's company. She is _____ about her job security.

   F nervous

   G confident

   H certain

   J happy

3 Please help me wash and _____ the dishes.

   A use

   B hide

   C dry

   D break

4 Anytime Dominic wanted to get a new _____, he went to the library.

   F hat

   G cell phone

   H book

   J car

5 Joelle had to save up for a long time. The car she wanted to buy was _____.

   A cheap

   B used

   C fuel-efficient

   D expensive

6 Manny and Frieda went to the _____ and had a picnic under the trees.

   F park

   G movies

   H restaurant

   J bank

7 Noah couldn't find his _____, so he didn't know what time it was.

   A keys

   B wallet

   C glasses

   D watch

8 Alan wanted to go on a tropical vacation, so he booked a trip to the _____.

   F mountains

   G city

   H beach

   J lake

Check your answers on page 79.

This passage is about frogs. Read the passage. Then do Numbers 1 through 5.

If you go for a drive through the country on a warm spring evening, you may be <u>fortunate</u> enough to hear frogs calling. However, you may not be so lucky. Ten years ago, there were many more frogs singing from ponds, streams, riverbanks, and ditches. Today this once <u>common</u> sound is heard less and less.

Worldwide, there are <u>fewer</u> frogs today than there were ten years ago. Though we do know some of the reasons for this problem, we don't know all of the reasons. In the last ten years, more than 170 different kinds of frogs have died out <u>completely</u>. Unless we take immediate action, even more are <u>doomed</u> to disappear forever.

1 Which of these words means the <u>opposite</u> of *fortunate* as it is used in this passage?

A lucky

B unlucky

C surprised

D wealthy

2 The passage says that the sound of frogs singing was once common. *Common* means about the same as

F ordinary

G rare

H unusual

J scary

3 Which of these words means the <u>opposite</u> of *fewer* as it is used in this passage?

A less

B smaller

C larger

D more

4 The passage says some types of frogs have died out completely. *Completely* means about the same as

F partly

G slowly

H quickly

J totally

5 The passage says that more types of frogs are doomed to disappear forever. In this context, *doomed* means about the same thing as

A unlikely

B doubtful

C certain

D possibly

Here is a list of steps to help you learn how to save money. Read the steps. Then do Numbers 6 through 9.

1. Keep a record of what you spend. Record everything, whether it is large or <u>minor</u>. When you keep this record, you'll see where your money is going.

2. Write a budget. You may think it is not <u>necessary</u> to write a budget, but doing this step will help you remember all your expenses.

3. Put something aside from every check. Even if it is a small amount, don't touch it. Your savings will grow if you keep adding to it. Don't <u>waste</u> your money; one day you will be glad you have it for something you need.

4. Decide what matters. You can't do everything, so decide what is most important. If you understand your <u>main</u> goals, you'll be able to sort out the little things from the big things.

5. Plan. Try to look ahead and decide what you will need next week, next month, and next year. Planning for the future is better than spending everything in the moment.

6 The passage says to keep track of minor purchases. *Minor* means about the same as

F big

G important

H small

J noticeable

7 The passage says you may think writing a budget isn't necessary. *Necessary* means about the same as

A needed

B optional

C voluntary

D helpful

8 Which of these words means the opposite of *waste* as it is used in this passage?

F save

G spend

H use

J pay

9 The passage says it's helpful to understand your main financial goals. *Main* means about the same as

A least important

B most important

C unimportant

D somewhat important

Read each item. Then do Numbers 10 through 17.

10 Sienna had to squint in the bright morning sun because she had forgotten her _____.

   F jacket

   G swim suit

   H car keys

   J sunglasses

11 Joaquin's boss was angry with him because he was late for a _____.

   A doctors' appointment

   B meeting

   C dinner

   D movie

12 Gracie needed to mail a letter. She looked in her desk for a _____.

   F ruler

   G mailman

   H stamp

   J post office

13 Please put your _____ clothes in the washing machine.

   A dirty

   B clean

   C new

   D folded

14 Lorna knew someone was calling her because she could hear her _____ ringing.

   F television

   G cell phone

   H alarm clock

   J microwave

15 Micah put together a crib for the new nursery. His wife was going to have a _____.

   A party

   B baby

   C wedding

   D meeting

16 Ali's feet hurt. She decided to take off her _____.

   F shoes

   G glasses

   H jewelry

   J gloves

17 Simone loves to eat fruit. Her favorite snack is _____.

   A apples

   B broccoli

   C cheese

   D pudding

Check your answers on pages 79–80.

Lesson 10 Details

Details are key facts, examples, or reasons supporting the main ideas of a reading passage. Details give you more information about the main idea and make the passage more interesting. Most details tell *who*, *what*, *when*, *why*, or *how*. Be sure to read details carefully.

Example **Read this passage about tractors. Look at the chart that shows the details of the passage. What was big, slow, and expensive?** _____

Farm tractors have been around since the late 1800s, but many farmers didn't use them until the mid-1900s. Early tractors were big, slow, and expensive. These loud and dangerous machines were not suited for small farms. Farmers did not have enough money to buy tractors, and also worried about how to fix them. Many farmers still used horses to do most of the heavy work. Later tractors became smaller, faster, and more affordable so that all farmers could use them.

Look at the chart. It shows the details for *who*, *where*, *when*, and *why*. Fill in the box for *what*.

Who	What	Where	When	Why/How
farmers		farms	late 1800s to mid-1900s	big, slow, expensive; not suited for small farms

Did you write *early tractors*? The passage says that early tractors were big, slow, and expensive.

Test Example

Read this passage about farming after Word War II. Then do Number 1.

Farming changed after World War II. In the late 1940s, soldiers returned to their farms. They had seen machines at work in war. The older farmers were leaving the fields. The younger farmers wanted the new machines, and tractor makers were ready to sell them. The "Golden Age" of American farm tractors began.

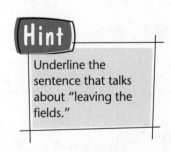

Hint

Underline the sentence that talks about "leaving the fields."

1   Who was leaving the fields?

A   soldiers

B   younger farmers

C   older farmers

D   all farmers

1 C The passage says that "The older farmers were leaving the fields." The soldiers (option A) and young farmers (option B) were returning to farms, not leaving them. Option D is incorrect because some farmers were leaving the fields while others were returning.

Practice

This is a passage about farm tractors in America. Read this passage. Then do Numbers 1 through 4.

The great age of American farm tractors lasted from about 1950 to 1970. Today many people collect the old tractors from this time period. These tractors are now antiques. Lovers of "Old Iron" range from seniors who used them when they were young to the people who remember seeing them when they were children. Allis-Chalmers, Oliver, Ford, Co-op, Avery, and Massey-Ferguson are the names of companies that used to make tractors. These tractors are no longer made.

Some people collect antique tractors. Two of the most-collected brands of tractors are John Deere and International Farmall. Everyone knows the green paint of John Deere. Anyone who has heard the old green machines also knows why these tractors are called "Johnny Poppers." However, some people are loyal to the bright red International Farmalls. The two groups are friendly rivals.

1 Which two brands are most-collected?

A Oliver and Ford

B Avery and Co-op

C John Deere and International Farmall

D Allis-Chalmers and Ford

2 Which tractor is bright red?

F Oliver

G Allis-Chalmers

H John Deere

J International Farmall

3 Which type of tractor is called "Johnny Popper"?

A International Farmall

B Allis-Chalmer

C John Deere

D Ford

4 Which time period is the great age of American farm tractors?

F 1800 to 1850

G 1850 to 1870

H 1900 to 1950

J 1950 to 1970

Check your answers on page 80.

Lesson 11   Sequence

Sequence is the order in which events happen. As you read, understanding sequence will help you recall information. Special words help you to understand the sequence of events. Some common sequence words include *first, to begin, next, then, after that,* and *finally.*

Example   **Read this passage. List the sequence words:**

_____

> Here's the best way to make a hard-boiled egg. First, place the eggs in a pot. Fill the pot with cold water that comes one inch above the eggs. Then heat the eggs until the water boils rapidly. After the water comes to a boil, remove the pot from the heat. Next, let the eggs sit in the hot water for 20–22 minutes. Finally, cool the eggs in cold water. This will stop them from further cooking.

Did you list *First, Then, After, Next,* and *Finally?* These words tell you the order in which each event happens.

Test Example

Read this passage about running errands. Then do Number 1.

> Janis ran many errands yesterday. First, she had to drop her sister off at school. Since the pharmacy was close by, she went there next. Then Janis went to the grocery store to pick up some bread. When she finally got home, Janis took a nap.

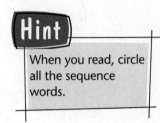

Hint

When you read, circle all the sequence words.

1 When did Janis go the grocery store?

   A before she dropped her sister off

   B after she took a nap

   C before she went to the pharmacy

   D after she went to the pharmacy

1 D The word *then* indicates that Janis went to the grocery store after she went to the pharmacy. She couldn't have gone to the store before she dropped off her sister (option A) because that happened first. The nap (option B) was the last event. She went to the grocery store after, not before (option C), she went to the pharmacy.

This list tells how to wash a car. Read the list. Then do Numbers 1 through 4.

Washing a Car

1. Choose a shady spot. Then make sure the doors and windows are closed.
2. Put one capful of soap in a bucket and fill the bucket with water.
3. Use a hose to spray off any dirt on the car. Start at the top of the car. Spray the tires last.
4. Dip a sponge or cloth into the soap-filled bucket. Wash one side of the car with the soapy sponge or cloth. Once the car is soapy, spray off the suds with a hose.
5. Repeat these steps on all four sides of the car. After that, give the car one final rinse.
6. Dry the car with a soft towel.

1 What should you do right after you choose a shady spot?

A dry the car

B fill a bucket with water

C make sure the doors and windows are closed

D use a soapy sponge or cloth to wash the car

2 What happens before you spray off the suds with a hose?

F dry the car

G wash one side of the car

H do the final rinse

J repeat the steps

3 When do you use a hose to spray off any dirt?

A before you fill a bucket with water

B after you wash one side

C before you find a shady spot

D after you fill a bucket with water

4 What comes after giving the car a final rinse?

F dry the car with a soft towel

G spray the tires

H choose a shady spot

J make sure the doors and windows are closed

Check your answers on page 80.

Lesson 12 | Stated Concepts

A stated concept is a key idea or statement that appears in a reading passage. A stated concept helps the reader understand the passage. It may explain something, support an idea, or tell why something is important.

Example **Read this passage about newspapers. Why don't most people depend on the newspaper to get their news?** _____

> People don't depend on newspapers to get the news anymore. Most people get the news from television. Now television brings the news to people 24 hours per day. Some people get their news from the Internet. Others listen to the radio. It is clear that fewer people are reading newspapers.

Did you write *most people get their news from television*? The second sentence states that most people get their news from television. Since this information is given directly in the passage, it is a stated concept.

Test Example

Read this passage about newspapers. Then do Number 1.

> Newspapers are in trouble, so they are taking steps to stay in business. To pull through these hard times, they are trying to cut costs. Many newspaper companies have had to lay off workers. Some papers have become smaller by offering fewer pages. Will these cuts be enough to keep them going?

1 What are newspaper companies doing to stay in business?

   A   They are cutting their ads.

   B   They are cutting their costs.

   C   They are using more technology.

   D   They are hiring more people.

1 B   The second sentence states that newspapers are trying to cut costs to stay in business. Options A and C are incorrect because the passage doesn't talk about ads or technology. Option D is incorrect because newspapers are cutting their workers, not hiring more workers.

Read this passage about how newspapers make money and attract readers. Then do Numbers 1 and 2.

To cover their costs and make money, newspaper companies sell ads. The cost of an ad is based on the size of the ad and the number of readers. To get more readers, newspapers are changing both the amount of news and the type of news articles. Many articles have less information and more photos. Readers like to see photos, but the photos take space away from other news.

1 Why do newspapers add more photos to articles?

A to sell ads

B to cut costs

C to get more readers

D to get fewer readers

2 What is the cost of an ad based on?

F how many articles there are in the paper

G the number of photos on the page

H the page it is on

J its size and the number of readers

Read this passage about the different sections of newspapers. Then do Numbers 3 and 4.

Newspapers have different sections for different kinds of news. Newspaper sections include local, national, and world news, as well as lifestyle and sports highlights. Readers enjoy local news and lifestyle sections, so newspapers make these sections larger. These sections have more ads than the national and world news sections because businesses want to place their ads in the sections that most people read.

3 Why do businesses want to place their ads in the local news and lifestyle sections?

A because they don't like world news

B because it costs less

C because most people read these sections

D because no one reads these sections

4 Which sections are larger in a local newspaper?

F the sports highlights

G the national and world news

H the local news and lifestyle sections

J the classifieds

Check your answers on page 80.

This is a passage about electric cars. Read the passage. Then do Numbers 1 through 4.

The electric car is not a new idea. As far back as the early 1900s, electric cars were in American cities. These early cars were popular. They were clean and quiet. In fact, they were great for the small roads in towns and cities. However, they couldn't be used to travel very far.

At the same time, there were also early cars that ran on gasoline. These cars were noisy, and they were often hard to start. They cost more to buy and to run because of the high price of oil and gas.

1 How long have electric cars been around?

   A since the early 1800s

   B since gas cars started breaking down a lot

   C since gas prices rose steeply

   D since the early 1900s

2 What was one problem with the early electric car?

   F It was quiet.

   G It cost too much.

   H It couldn't go very far.

   J It had fewer parts.

3 According to the passage, what was wrong with early cars that ran on gas?

   A They made no noise.

   B They were hard to start.

   C They couldn't travel very far.

   D They often needed new parts.

4 Which is true about electric cars?

   F They have never been popular.

   G They use a lot of energy.

   H They are hard to drive.

   J They are not a new idea.

Read this passage about the Civil War. Then do Numbers 5 through 8.

The Civil War took place between 1861 and 1865. It was a terrible time in American history. In 1861 Abraham Lincoln became president. When he took office, many states in the South left the Union. After that, war broke out.

At first, it seemed that the South might win the war. Troops from the North were not ready. Lincoln believed the North could win even though they had lost many battles. He called for more troops. By the fall of 1862, the war was a bloody struggle. It was not clear who would win.

Then the North began to win more battles. The South, which had fewer men and arms, could not keep up.

In July of 1863, the two armies fought at the Battle of Gettsyburg. General Lee of the South was forced to pull back. In April 1865, Lee surrendered to Grant in Virginia, proving the North was strong in the end. The war was over.

5 What happened before the Battle of Gettsyburg?

A The South pulled back.

B The war ended.

C Lincoln became president.

D General Lee surrendered.

6 Which event happened first?

F The South looked as if it might win.

G Lincoln called for more troops.

H Lee surrendered to Grant.

J The North began to win more battles.

7 What happened in April 1865?

A the Battle of Gettysburg

B Lincoln called for more troops.

C Northern troops were not ready.

D Lee surrendered to Grant.

8 Which of the following statements is accurate?

F The North won the war quickly.

G The South had more men and arms.

H The North was strong in the end.

J The South won after a bloody struggle.

Read this passage about the trucking business. Then do Numbers 9 through 12.

Have you ever noticed how many big trucks there are on the road? About 80% of products in the United States travel by truck. More companies use trucks to get things to market than any other way.

The trucking business is not easy. High fuel prices mean it is expensive to haul products. These costs get passed to buyers. That's one reason prices have gone up for many of the things you buy.

There other ways to haul products that cost less than trucks. For example, trains carry things cheaply. A long line of rail cars can carry more than a truck for less money. Ships and boats also carry things cheaply. However, trains and ships cannot travel everywhere. They cannot go from door to door. Someone still has to carry goods from a station to a store.

On the other hand, trucks can go almost anywhere. Also, trucks carry things faster than trains and ships. For companies that must get things to market on time and without problems, trucks are the best choice.

9 How do most companies get their products to market in the United States?

A by trains

B by trucks

C by air freight

D by ships

10 How much U.S. product is moved using trucks?

F about 10%

G about 50%

H about 80%

J 100%

11 Which statement is true about using trains to carry products?

A Trains can go door to door.

B Trains are faster than trucks.

C Trains do not require fuel.

D Trains carry loads more cheaply than trucks.

12 What is one challenge for trucking companies?

F Trucks go too slow.

G Trucks are too small.

H There are not enough roads.

J Fuel prices are very high.

Check your answers on pages 80–81.

Lesson 13 Character Aspects

Certain clues tell you what kind of person a character is in a reading passage. Ask yourself, what do the details in the reading passage tell me about each person or character? Why does a person or character think or act as he or she does?

Example: **Read this passage about Vincent van Gogh. How do you think Vincent van Gogh felt about nature and the world around him?**

Vincent van Gogh made a study of the world that he saw. He made bright and colorful paintings of the things around him. Some of his paintings showed yellow sunflowers in pots or strong country people. He sensed the spirit of the countryside. He used bright colors to make his works come to life.

You can see that Vincent van Gogh was probably sensitive to nature and the world around him. The passage says he used sunflowers in his paintings, often painted the things around him, painted country people as strong, and "sensed the spirit of the countryside." These statements show that van Gogh was sensitive to nature and his surroundings.

Test Example

Read the passage about Frido Kahlo. Then do Number 1.

Frida Kahlo was a famous artist from Mexico who died at the age of 47. She had very bad health problems throughout her life, which she tried to overcome. Kahlo painted many self-portraits. Many of her paintings showed the pain and suffering she felt in her life. They also showed her pride in her Mexican-Indian culture. Her paintings give many people hope.

1 What do Frida's self-portraits say about her?

A She was a very happy person.

B She didn't think much about others.

C She had been through hard times in her life.

D She didn't like her country.

1 **C** Frida painted many sad things about herself, so she had probably had a hard life. Option A is incorrect because her portraits show sadness. Option B is incorrect; there is no information in the passage to support this. Option D is the opposite of how she feels about her country.

Practice

This is a passage about Henri Matisse. Read the passage. Then do Numbers 1 and 2.

Henri Matisse was born in France in 1869. He went to school to study law, mainly because his father wanted him to. He started painting as a young adult while he was healing from being sick. His mother brought him art supplies to keep him busy at home. Henri later said, "I threw myself into it like a beast that plunges toward the thing he loves."

Henri Matisse also sculpted, but he is best known for his colorful and bold paintings. Henri studied other artists. Their works gave him ideas. Some of Henri's work was laughed at when he first showed it. This did not stop Henri from making art. Many people outside of France thought his work was amazing. It wasn't until after he died in 1954 that the people of France understood how great his artwork really is.

1 Henri said, "I threw myself into it like a beast that plunges toward the thing he loves." What does this say about Henri and how he felt about art?

A He put everything into his artwork and loved it.

B He wanted to throw out the supplies and thought it was dumb.

C He got mad and didn't want to do it.

D He painted a little but didn't really like it.

2 Henri still made art even though some of his work was laughed at. He must be

F angry

G weak

H determined

J shy

Check your answers on page 81.

Lesson 14 Main Idea

The main idea of a paragraph is the most important point of what you are reading. All of the sentences in a paragraph support, or give more information about, the main idea.

Example: **Read the following passage. Look for the main idea. What is the passage about?**

> Early in the twentieth century, Henry Ford began to make new cars in his automobile factory. He used a new way of making the cars. It allowed him to make the cars faster and for less money. This style quickly changed how cars were made. It also changed how factories made other things. Many factories followed Ford's lead.

This passage is about Henry Ford's method of making cars. All the sentences in the paragraph give more information about this new method: who invented it, what its benefits were, and what changes it led to.

Test Example

This is a passage about American car makers. Read the passage. Then do Number 1.

TABE Strategy

To figure out the main idea, ask yourself, "What is this passage about?"

> There have been many car companies in the United States since the early 1900s. Everyone knows about Ford Motor Company, but what about others? In the 1930s and 1940s, companies such as Nash Motors, Packard Motor Car Company, and Hudson Motor Car Company were popular. Smaller companies like these aren't in business anymore. By the 1970s, the largest car companies in the United States were Ford Motor Company, General Motors, and Chrysler. They were called "The Big Three." Who knows where these companies will be in the future and what new car companies we will see?

1 What is the main idea of this paragraph?

A The "Big Three" were the top car companies in the 1970s.

B Hudson Motor Car Company went out of business.

C Only big companies can sell cars in the U.S.

D The United States has had many car companies.

1 D The main idea is that there have been many different car companies in the United States. Options A and B are details about American car companies. Option C is not discussed in the passage.

Practice

The passages below are about cars in the 1950s. Read each passage. Then do Numbers 1 and 2.

The 1950s were the Golden Age of the automobile. Americans had fallen in love with cars. The cost of cars dropped, putting cars within reach of many more Americans than ever before. In addition, gas was very cheap. New and better roads were being built all over the country. This allowed families to really enjoy the cars they owned.

1 What is this passage mostly about?

A The 1950s were a good time for Americans and their cars.

B More roads were built in the 1950s.

C Car radios became common.

D Every family in the United States owned a car.

By the 1950s, cars had changed in many ways. They came in many different colors and were much bigger than before. Many cars had long tail fins. Other cars had shiny bumpers. Cars of that time were roomy inside, too. The seats were big and soft, which was good for long trips. People were proud of the way their cars looked and enjoyed all the new changes.

2 What is this passage mostly about?

F By the 1950s, cars went faster than before.

G By the 1950s, cars had soft seats.

H By the 1950s, cars had changed a lot.

J By the 1950s, cars had new, shiny bumpers.

Check your answers on page 81.

Lesson 15 Cause/Effect

A cause is the reason why something happens. An effect is what happens as a result of the cause. For example, if a driver falls asleep at the wheel (cause), the car may crash (effect). Note that an event may have more than one cause or more than one effect. Also, the effect of one event may turn into a cause for another event.

Example **Read this passage. Think about the cause and the end result. Which events in the passage are causes? What happens as a result of these events?**

> George had a bad day. He was looking forward to going home and resting. When he got to his door, he reached into his pocket for his keys. However, the keys weren't there. He looked in all his pockets and in his car. Finally he found an open window. He pushed it up and climbed into his house. When he put his feet on the floor, he noticed a big rip in the leg of his pants. George's day had gone from bad to terrible.

In this case, because George loses his keys, he can't unlock the door. Because he can't unlock the door, he climbs through a window. Because he climbs through a window, he rips his pants. It is a chain reaction of causes and effects.

Test Example

Read the passage about Richard and his library books. Then do Number 1.

> Richard likes to read. He often goes to the library to borrow books. One week he borrows four new books. He takes them home and starts to read. The next week, he is very busy at work. He has to work late, and on weekends. He doesn't have much time to read. He forgets to return the books on time. A month later, he gets a card in the mail. It is from the library. His books are past due. Now he owes money to the library.

Hint

To identify a cause, ask yourself, "Why did this happen?" To identify an effect, ask yourself, "What happened as a result of this situation?"

1 Why does Richard owe money to the library?

A He loses the library books.

B He doesn't return the books on time.

C He loses his library card.

D He wants to buy the books.

1 B Richard doesn't return the books on time. Because the books are late, he owes money to the library. Options A and C are incorrect because the passage doesn't say that he loses the books or his library card. Option D is incorrect because he borrowed books from the library; he did not buy them.

Practice

This is a passage about Joan and her garden. Read the passage. Then do Numbers 1 and 2.

Joan decided to plant a small garden. She dug up a spot in her yard. She raked over the soil and pulled out the rocks and weeds. Then she planted seeds for corn, peas, carrots, and beans. She planted the seeds in neat rows. It was hard work, but she looked forward to eating food from her own garden.

Every few days, she pulled out weeds. When the soil looked dry, she watered it. A few weeks later, some small, green leaves appeared. It seemed like magic. Joan was very happy to see that her garden was beginning to grow. Every week, the plants got taller. They looked healthy, and the area was beginning to look like a real garden. She couldn't wait to taste all the fresh vegetables.

1 Why did Joan dig up a spot in her yard?

A It was hard work, but she wanted to do it.

B She had decided to plant a small garden.

C She wanted to have a bigger garden than her neighbor.

D She wanted to bury a treasure.

2 What was the result of Joan's hard work in the garden?

F The plants grew to be strong and healthy.

G She couldn't eat all the vegetables.

H Heavy rain stopped the plants from growing.

J She started her own farmer's market.

Check your answers on page 81.

Lesson 16 Compare/Contrast

On the TABE, you will compare to find how information and values are the same. When you contrast information and values, you find how they are different. Comparing and contrasting information and values can help you better understand what you read.

Example   The chart below shows the vegetables that Melody planted and how often she should water them each week. Read the information in the chart.

Vegetable	Weekly Watering
Carrots	7 times
Tomatoes	2–3 times
Onions	1 time
Squash	2–3 times

Contrast the values. Which vegetable needs the most water?

_____

Compare the values. Which two vegetables need the same amount of water?

_____

Did you write *carrots* for the most water? *Most* is another way to say greatest. When you contrast the numbers, you find that 7 is the greatest value.

Did you write *tomatoes* and *squash* for the same amount? When you compare the numbers, you find that they are the same for tomatoes and squash. Both need water 2-3 times a week.

Test Example

Read the passage about how Julia and her brother Tom start their day. Then do Number 1.

Julia gets up every morning at 6 o'clock. She awakes on her own. She doesn't need an alarm clock. She likes to start the day early. Julia's brother Tom hates to wake up early. He would rather sleep until 10 o'clock. However, he has to get up at the same time as Julia to get ready for work. He needs a loud alarm clock to wake him up. Without it, he would always be late.

Hint

If questions asks how two things are alike, it is asking you how they are the same. You will need to compare.

1 Julia and Tom are alike because they both

  A wake up at 6 o'clock   C use alarm clocks

  B like to get up early   D enjoy sleeping late

1 A The passage states that Julia gets up at 6 o'clock and that her brother gets up at the same time. Julia likes to get up early, but Tom likes to sleep, so options B and D are incorrect. Option C is incorrect because Julia does not use an alarm clock.

The graph below shows the number of students in different types of art classes. Study the graph. Then do Numbers 1 and 2.

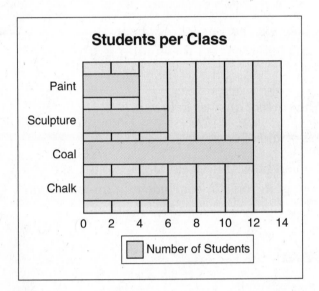

Students per Class

Paint
Sculpture
Coal
Chalk

0 2 4 6 8 10 12 14

☐ Number of Students

1 More students take sculpture than

A Paint

B Coal

C Chalk

D Ink

2 Which of these sentences about the art students is true?

F More students are taking Paint than Sculpture.

G Paint has more students than Chalk.

H There are more students in Sculpture than in Chalk.

J More students are taking Coal than any other class.

Read the items below. Then do Numbers 3 and 4.

3 Many people now use manual lawnmowers, which have no motor and are powered by human force. Unlike noisy gas-powered mowers, manual mowers are environmentally friendly and require no gas, but their sharp blades pose the same danger. Manual mowers are lighter and easier to push. They are cheaper to maintain than gas-powered mowers and make virtually no noise.

Manual mowers and gas-powered mowers are alike because they

A are noisy

B use gas

C have sharp blades

D are environmentally friendly

4 The table below shows the amount of time that Dylan spends doing 4 types of exercises each day.

Exercise	Time
Stretching	10 minutes
Walking	30 minutes
Weights	20 minutes
Jogging	10 minutes

Which two exercises does Dylan do for the same amount of time?

F Stretching and Walking

G Weights and Walking

H Jogging and Weights

J Jogging and Stretching

Check your answers on page 81.

Lesson 17 — Conclusions

While reading, it is natural to form conclusions. To form a conclusion, combine information from the passage with your own knowledge about people and the world. When you draw conclusions, it is important to make sure that the conclusions make sense.

Example **Read this passage about Anna.**

> Anna's parents are getting a dog. Anna is excited. She learns about ways to train and take care of a dog. Anna tells all of her friends at school that she is getting a dog.

What can you conclude about Anna? Circle the correct answer below.

> Anna loves dogs.   Anna is afraid of dogs.

Did you circle *Anna loves dogs*? Look for clues about how Anna feels. She is excited; she prepares to get a dog; and she tells all her friends about it. You can conclude that someone who acts this way must love dogs.

Test Example

Read this passage about Anna's choice in dogs. Then do Number 1.

> Anna's dad gives Anna a choice between a border collie and a golden retriever. He grew up on a farm where he had two border collies and a golden retriever. The border collies helped to herd the sheep on the farm. The golden retriever was a house pet. Anna's dad thinks both types of dogs are very friendly and good with children.

Hint

After you read the question, read the passage a second time. As you read, look for reasons why Anna's dad would choose those two types of dogs.

1 Anna's dad lets her choose between a golden retriever and a border collie because

   A he has heard that they are both nice dogs

   B a neighbor has both types for sale

   C these types are the only two dogs that Anna likes

   D he likes both kinds of dogs

---

1 **D** The paragraph says that Anna's dad grew up with border collies and a golden retriever, and he thinks they are friendly and good with children. From this information, you can conclude he likes them. He did not hear about them from someone else (option A). The passage does not mention neighbors (option B). Nothing in the passage says that Anna doesn't like other types of dogs (option C).

Practice

The passage below is about Anna and what type of dog she should get. Read the passage. Then do Numbers 1 and 2.

Anna reads that golden retrievers are calm and happy most of the time. They don't need a lot of space to play. Border collies are very lively and need lots of exercise every day in order to be well-behaved. Anna and her parents like to go to a nearby park where they ride bicycles, swim, and take hikes, but these activities are not easy to do with a dog. Anna thinks about their yard. It is small and has very little room for a dog to run.

1 The family's backyard is best suited for

A a border collie

B a golden retriever

C biking

D swimming

2 What can you conclude about Anna's family?

F They don't like to exercise.

G They don't like animals.

H They enjoy outdoor activities.

J They live on a farm.

Read the items below. Then do Numbers 3 and 4.

3 Therin walks her dog. She sits on a bench and listens to birds sing. She leaves when the sun goes down. Therin was most likely

A in a supermarket

B at a movie

C in a park

D on a plane

4 Dala is starting a dog-training class and created the ad below.

> ### Dog Training Classes
>
> Classes held every Thursday at Zilker Park. All dogs welcome—all breeds, all ages. Please visit our Web site for more information.

A person would most likely visit the website to learn

F what time the class begins

G where the class is located

H what day the class happens

J what kinds of dogs are allowed

Check your answers on page 81.

Level E

Lesson 17 • **49**

The passage below is about a famous volleyball player. Read the passage. Then do Numbers 1 and 2.

Gabrielle Reece is a well-known volleyball player. She played volleyball as a young adult and then went to college. Gabrielle went to Florida State University on a volleyball scholarship, where she led her team to several victories. She even turned down high-paying jobs to finish college. After college, Gabrielle played on many volleyball tours and became a successful professional volleyball player. She has won many awards and honors in her career and has competed in the Olympic games.

1 This passage is mostly about

A people who play volleyball

B the popularity of volleyball

C volleyball player Gabrielle Reece

D how to play volleyball

2 Gabrielle turned down jobs to finish college. What does this say about Gabrielle?

F She doesn't like to work.

G She wanted to play in the Olympics.

H She thought school was important.

J She was too shy to meet new people.

The passage below is about nutrition ads. Read the passage. Then do Numbers 3 and 4.

You probably hear messages and see ads every day about nutrition products. This is because businesses want you to buy their products. Some of these products are healthy, but many are not. Although it can be difficult to sort through all the information, there are a few rules to help you have a healthy diet.

First eat a variety of fruits and vegetables. This will ensure you get a variety of different nutrients. Avoid fats, added sugars, and salt. These can impact your health in a negative way. Eating right will make you feel good and will reduce your risk for diseases like diabetes, heart disease, and certain cancers.

3 What is one effect of eating a variety of fruits and vegetables?

A ensures you get a variety of nutrients

B increases your risk of disease

C impacts your health in a negative way

D helps you remember the rules for healthy eating

4 Businesses create ads and messages about nutrition products because they want you to

F be healthy

G buy their products

H live longer

J start your own business

This passage is about Andrew's cell phone. Read the passage. Then do Numbers 5 through 9.

When Andrew entered high school, his parents said he could get a cell phone. Andrew promised his parents that he would only use his cell phone for very important things. He would call home when he was going to be late or when he needed a ride. Andrew's parents would pay the bill for the cell phone. They warned him not to go over his monthly minutes.

At first things went well. Andrew kept his promise. After one month, some problems came up. He was talking on his phone too much, and he used more than his monthly minutes. In addition, his social studies teacher got mad at him because Andrew was texting in class. Andrew's parents were not pleased.

5 Why are Andrew's parents not pleased?
   A Andrew stayed out late and did not call his parents.
   B Andrew wouldn't pay his bill on time.
   C Andrew used his phone too much.
   D Andrew called home too much.

6 Why does Andrew's social studies teacher get mad?
   F Andrew got a bad grade on a test.
   G Andrew forgot his homework.
   H Andrew answered his phone in class.
   J Andrew was texting in class.

7 What is this passage mostly about?
   A Andrew's use of his new cell phone
   B how Andrew loves his phone
   C why Andrew's social studies teacher got angry
   D why Andrew's parents got him a cell phone

8 How could Andrew be described?
   F He breaks the law.
   G He is a good student.
   H He likes talking on the phone.
   J He always keeps his promises.

9 Andrew's cell phone bill is probably
   A in the mail box
   B unpaid
   C expensive
   D going to be late

The graph below shows the number of cookbooks sold each month at a bookstore. Study the graph. Then do Numbers 10 and 11.

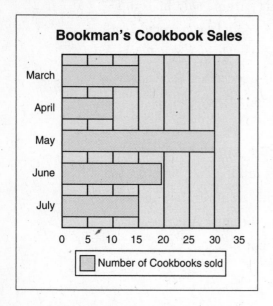

Bookman's Cookbook Sales

Number of Cookbooks sold

10 More cookbooks were sold in July than in

F March

G April

H May

J June

11 Which of these sentences about Bookman's cookbook sales is true?

A More cookbooks were sold in April than in July.

B May had the fewest cookbook sales.

C Fewer cookbooks were sold in March than in April.

D March and July had the same sales.

12 Tessa turns on her computer. She sits at her desk and writes an e-mail. She answers the phone and talks to a customer. She waves hello to a co-worker. Tessa is most likely

F studying at a library

G working in an office

H directing traffic

J writing a symphony

Read the flyer below about Yoga classes. Then do Numbers 13 and 14.

> **Mommy-To-Be Yoga Classes**
> Come join one of our classes for expectant mothers. You can use yoga to help you relax. Classes happen every day at 1:00 p.m. and 5:00 p.m. Each class has poses that are good for beginning, intermediate, and advanced yoga moms. Classes start at $15. Call our studio for more details.

13 What is the flyer mostly about?

A yoga classes for expectant moms

B beginning yoga poses

C relaxation for expectant moms

D a yoga studio

14 A person would most likely call the studio to learn

F what time the classes begin

G where the studio is located

H what day the classes happen

J who the classes are for

Read the passage below. Then do Numbers 15 and 16.

A muskrat is a type of rodent. Muskrats have narrow tails and are often seen in the daytime. Most of the time, muskrats eat plants, but mostly, they eat fish or frogs.

A beaver is another type of rodent. Beavers only eat plants. They have wide, flat tails that help them swim, and they do most of their work at night.

Both beavers and muskrats are excellent swimmers. They can swim on the surface and below the water. Generally, neither animal likes humans. Beavers cut down trees by using their teeth. This is how they get wood to build their dams. Muskrats do not build dams, and they don't cut down trees.

15 Which environment is best suited for beavers and muskrats?

   A the dry desert

   B a ship on the ocean

   C a river near a forest

   D a residential neighborhood

16 Beavers and muskrats both

   F have flat tails

   G build dams

   H eat fish and frogs

   J are types of rodents

Read the passage below. Then do Number 17.

Abraham Lincoln was the president of the United States during the Civil War. The southern states wanted to leave the United States, but Lincoln did not want the country to be divided. He wanted to keep one strong nation. He fought to make sure that the states stayed together as one country. He is often thought of as one of the greatest presidents. He was wise, and he was able to learn from his mistakes. The United States would be a very different place today if not for Abraham Lincoln.

17 Which of these best describes Lincoln as a president?

   A He was mean and selfish.

   B He loved his country.

   C He was a great writer.

   D He pushed people around.

The table below shows when to introduce some foods into a baby's diet. Study the table. Then do Number 18.

Food	Introduce at
Green beans	7–8 months
Mashed beans	6–9 months
Plain yogurt	8–12 months
Rice cereal	4–7 months
Squash	7–8 months

18 Which two foods have the same introduction times?

   F Green beans and Mashed beans

   G Plain yogurt and Rice cereal

   H Green beans and Squash

   J Squash and Plain yogurt

Check your answers on pages 81–82.

Lesson 18 ▸ Fact/Opinion

Facts and opinions are two kinds of statements. What's the difference between them? Statements that can be proven are facts. Statements that can't be proven, or that other people may disagree with, are opinions.

Example **Read this passage about Hawaii. Then answer the questions that follow.**

> Hawaii is the fiftieth state. It is made up of eight major islands. The largest island is called *Hawaii*. This island is also known as the "Big Island." It is also the most beautiful island.

Which of these two statements is a <u>fact</u> about the Big Island?

1. It is the largest of the Hawaiian Islands.

2. It is the most beautiful of the Hawaiian Islands.

Did you choose the first statement? Some people may think the Big Island is the most beautiful island, but this is an opinion. It is a statement that cannot be proven; others may disagree with this idea. It can be proven that Hawaii is the largest of the islands. This statement is a fact.

Test Example

Read this passage about the Big Island. Then do Number 1.

> Hawaii is a land of many contrasts. The island has mountains with active volcanoes. It has rain forests and deserts. It also has lots of open spaces. These lands are home to the best cattle ranches in the world.

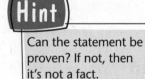

Hint

Can the statement be proven? If not, then it's not a fact.

1 Which of these statements is an <u>opinion</u>?

A The island has mountains with active volcanoes.

B The island has lots of open spaces.

C The island's cattle ranches are the best in the world.

D The island has rain forests and deserts.

1 C The word *best* states an opinion. It can't be proven. The other options are facts. They can be proven. The island does have mountains with active volcanoes. It has open spaces. It has rain forests and deserts.

Read this passage about the Big Island of Hawaii. Study the map. Then do Numbers 1 and 2.

The beautiful Big Island is home to two mountains: Mauna Loa, which means "long mountain," and Mauna Kea, which means "white mountain." The taller of the two is Mauna Kea. Many visitors come to the Big Island to see the mountains and to see Kilauea, an active volcano on the side of Mauna Loa in Volcanoes National Park. On rainy nights, the volcano is an amazing sight.

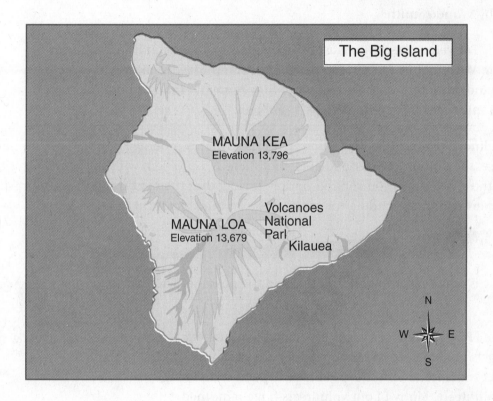

1 Which of these statements is an <u>opinion</u> about the Big Island?

  A Mauna Kea means "white mountain."

  B The island has two major mountains.

  C Kilauea is an active volcano.

  D Kilauea is an amazing sight on rainy nights.

2 Which of these statements is a <u>fact</u> about the Big Island?

  F The Big Island is beautiful.

  G Mauna Kea is taller than Mauna Loa.

  H The mountains and volcano are the only things worth seeing on the Big Island.

  J The middle of the Big Island is the most exciting part.

Check your answers on page 83.

Lesson 19 | Predict Outcomes

Questions on the TABE will ask you to decide what event is likely to happen next in a reading passage. The more closely you read, the better you will understand the text. The better you understand the text, the more often your predictions will be correct.

Example This passage is from a letter that was printed in a community newsletter. Read the passage. What idea will probably come in the next sentence?

> **We Count on You**
> by Wanda Smith
>
> For years, the senior class at Lakeville High School has taken a trip to Washington, DC. The students have fun and learn a lot. Many students later say this trip is what they remember most about their senior year. This year, there is a problem.

The headline "We Count on You" shows that the writer is probably going to ask for help. In the last sentence, the author tells her audience that there is a problem with the yearly senior class trip. Using these two clues, you can reasonably predict that the next thing the author will do is ask her audience for help sending the senior class on their class trip.

Test Example

This passage is about a youth golf league. Read the passage. Then do Number 1.

The FP Youth Golf League is made up of volunteers. No one gets paid to keep our group going. The only money we collect is the fee to join the group. We depend completely on volunteers. Many of our volunteers have remained with the league even after their own children were too old to play. Now, however, some of them need to move on. In the near future, we will not have enough volunteers to run the league. We need help finding new volunteers to take over key jobs.

TABE Strategy

To predict what might happen next when reading, look for *time-related* statements.

1 What will probably happen if the league doesn't get new volunteers?

 A The league might end.

 B The league will go on forever.

 C All of the present volunteers will stay.

 D Some of the present volunteers will quit.

1 A The article says the league completely depends on its volunteers to keep the group going. The article stresses how important they are to the group. Without them, the league could end. Option B is incorrect. The group can't go on forever if there aren't enough people to do key jobs. Option C is incorrect. The article says that some of the present volunteers need to leave the league. Option D is incorrect. There is nothing in the article to suggest that volunteers will quit if new volunteers are not found.

Read this passage about different types of cameras. Then do Numbers 1 through 3.

When Daria's father passed away, Daria learned that he had left her his expensive camera in his will. It was an old film camera, not a new digital one that everyone used these days. It had two long, expensive-looking lenses: one for shooting small objects close up, and one for shooting objects far way.

Daria had never had a film camera. She had always taken pictures of her two children with a small, inexpensive digital camera. But she had also been disappointed with the quality of her photos. She knew that her dad had taken incredible photos using this older camera. Her daughter's birthday was coming up, and Daria wanted to take great pictures of the celebration. She also knew that the photography store down the street offered lessons about how to use film cameras effectively.

1 What will probably happen next?

A Daria will bake a cake for her daughter's birthday party.

B Daria will pack away her father's old camera.

C Daria will buy a new digital camera.

D Daria will take lessons on how to use the old film camera.

2 What will Daria probably do with the film camera's two lenses?

F pack them away with the camera

G sell them to a professional photographer

H learn how to use them with the film camera

J throw them away because they are so old

3 What will Daria probably use to take pictures at her daughter's birthday party?

A the old film camera

B her regular digital camera

C a new digital camera

D a video recorder

Check your answers on page 83.

Read the passage about voting. Then do Numbers 1 and 2.

Every year, citizens all over the United States go to the polls to vote for people they think would do a good job at running the city, state, or even country. This happens on the first Tuesday in November, which is also known as Election Day.

The people who earn the most votes win the election. However, many citizens do not go out and vote. They think that their vote doesn't matter, but some elections can be very close. Just a few votes can sometimes change the result of an election. That is why it is important to vote. Every vote counts.

1 Which sentence is a <u>fact</u>?

   A It is important to vote.

   B Voting doesn't matter.

   C Only good people run for election.

   D The United States holds elections every year.

2 Which sentence is an <u>opinion</u>?

   F Election Day is the first Tuesday in November.

   G Voting is important.

   H Voters decide the winners of the elections.

   J Some elections can be very close.

This passage is about electing our first African-American president. Read the passage. Then do Numbers 3 and 4.

In November 2008, Barack Obama won the election for president of the United States. Obama made history by winning the presidential race. He became the first African-American president of the United States. All other American presidents have been white men. The 2008 election was the most important presidential election in U.S. history.

Historically, African Americans have had to struggle to get the same rights as other citizens. Because of this history of inequality, many people did not believe that a black man could become president. When Obama said he was going to run for president, many people thought it would be impossible for him to win. President Obama proved them wrong.

3 Which sentence is an <u>opinion</u>?

   A African Americans have had a history of inequality.

   B Barack Obama is the first African-American president.

   C The 2008 election was the most important U.S. election ever.

   D Until 2008, American presidents were always white men.

4 Which of these statements is a <u>fact</u>?

   F African Americans make great presidents.

   G Barack Obama was elected in 2008.

   H Everyone wanted Barack Obama to win the election.

   J African Americans have had to struggle more than anyone else.

Read this passage about the Robinson family. Then do Numbers 5 and 6.

Mr. and Mrs. Robinson have six children. With such a big family, money is always a problem. Most weeks, they spend between $300.00 and $350.00 on food. This week, however, they have a bit of a problem. Last week, they had to have a new water heater put into their house, so they don't have much money. This week, the most they can spend on food is $250.00.

Mr. Robinson likes his job, but he often worries about money. Mr. Robinson's boss offered Mr. Robinson a different job that pays more money. However, the work will not be as interesting as his current work. Mr. Robinson must decide whether or not to take the new job.

5 What will Mr. Robinson probably decide about the job offer?

   A He will probably remain in his old job.

   B He will probably take the new job.

   C He will probably look for a new job.

   D He will probably become a stay-at-home parent.

6 What would probably happen if Mr. Robinson were given a $100 bonus?

   F He would buy food for his family.

   G He would buy a new cell phone.

   H He would buy a new suit for work.

   J He would buy a new water heater.

This is a passage about Jennifer's camping trip. Read the passage. Then do Numbers 7 and 8.

Jennifer is looking for a summer job. She has a special reason for needing money. Jennifer wants to go on a camping trip with some friends. Jennifer needs to earn some money so that she can help with the cost of camping gear and supplies. She also has to pay part of the fee for a rental space for the tent at a state park.

Jennifer notices that the landscapers who cut people's grass in her neighborhood always seem very busy. Jennifer has always enjoyed working in her own yard and has been in charge of mowing it for years. This gives her an idea.

7 What will Jennifer probably do to earn money?

A extra chores around the house

B work in a restaurant

C mow other people's lawns

D sell all her camping gear

8 Is it likely that Jennifer will be able to go camping?

F No—there will not be enough work for her to do.

G No—she does not want to work during the summer.

H Yes—she will earn enough money mowing lawns.

J Yes—her parents will give her the money she needs.

Check your answers on page 83.

Performance Assessment
Reading

The Reading Performance Assessment is identical to the actual TABE in format and length. It will give you an idea of what the real test is like. Allow yourself 50 minutes to complete this assessment. Check your answers on pages 83–86.

Sample A

Cody always set her _____ so she would get up on time in the morning.

A alarm

B stove

C mirror

D door

Sample B

Aaron was on his way to work. He was on time and ready for the day. He looked out the car window and saw the sky growing darker. Then Aaron saw lightning and heard thunder. *I'll just have to run to the door,* he thought. *Maybe it won't last all day.*

What item is Aaron missing?

F watch

G lunch

H umbrella

J keys

Page 63

Go On ▶

This a recipe for macaroni and cheese. Read the recipe. Then do Numbers 1 though 6.

You are bound to love this recipe for macaroni and cheese, and it's not hard to make either. Most people use cheddar cheese, but you can use American, colby, Swiss, or a mixture of cheese as well!

Grated cheese, 8 ounces   Milk, 2 cups

Elbow macaroni, 1 ½ cups   Optional: salt or pepper

Butter or margarine, ¼ cup

Fill a large pot with about 1½ quarts of water and bring the water to a boil.

Add the macaroni to the pot and cook on medium heat for 7 to 10 minutes. Turn the heat down if the pot starts to boil over.

When the macaroni is cooked, drain the water.

Put the drained macaroni back into the pot.

Stir in butter or margarine, milk, and grated cheese.

Mix until cheese has melted.

Add salt and pepper to taste.

1 Which of these statements is an <u>opinion</u>?

A You can use a mixture of cheeses.

B The dish is not hard to make.

C You need two cups of milk.

D Adding salt and pepper is optional.

2 This passage describes salt and pepper as optional. *Optional* means about the same as

F recipe

G unnecessary

H kitchen

J required

3 What should you do as soon as the macaroni is cooked?

A Drain the water.

B Put macaroni back into the pot.

C Mix until cheese has melted.

D Add salt and pepper to taste.

4 If the pot starts to boil over, you should

F turn off the heat

G turn up the heat

H stir the water

J turn down the heat

5 What is the final step in the recipe?

A Bring the water to a boil.

B Add salt and pepper to taste.

C Bake at 350°.

D Add butter, milk, and cheese.

6 Which word means the <u>opposite of</u> *bound* as it is used in the note at the top of the recipe?

F walk

G border

H unlikely

J free

This graph shows the favorite sports of the members of Hill Country Gym. Study the graph. Then do Numbers 7 through 10.

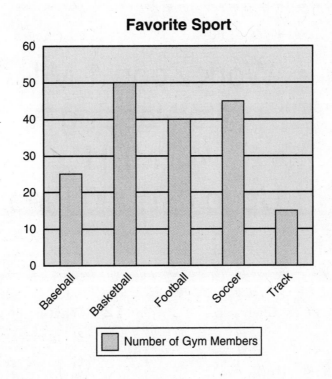

Favorite Sport

Number of Gym Members

7 How many Hill Country Gym members like baseball the best?

A 20

B 25

C 40

D 50

8 Which sport is the least favorite among Hill Country Gym members?

F baseball

G football

H soccer

J track

9 Based on the graph, which of the following statements is true?

A Fewer people like basketball than baseball.

B Fewer people like soccer than football.

C More people like baseball than track.

D More people like football than basketball.

10 If Hill Country Gym hosted a tournament for one of the sports, which would most likely have the most people participate?

F baseball

G basketball

H football

J soccer

Work Zone 1 Mile
No Passing
45 MPH
Up to $1,000 Fine

11 Where would you most likely see this sign?

A in an office

B at city hall

C in a park

D on a highway

12 What is the purpose of this sign?

F to give a warning

G to describe a scene

H to tell about a job

J to tell a story

Go On ▶

This is a passage about armadillos. Read the passage. Then do Numbers 13 through 17.

Armadillos are amazing animals. They have been around for a very long time. The shell of an armadillo is made of bone, so most armadillos cannot roll into a ball. They have short legs, but they can run surprisingly fast.

Armadillos are expert diggers. They dig for their food. They have strong claws that help them tear through the ground or old wood to find food. Armadillos eat mostly beetles, grubs, and other insects, but they will also eat dead flesh and a few plants.

Armadillos cannot stand the cold because they have very little fat. They live mostly in places that are warm year round. However, in the last hundred years, they have spread northward. In the United States, they have been seen as far north as Illinois. Some people think that they are traveling farther north because of the changing climate all over in the world.

Armadillos may be disappearing, though. People and dogs are harming them. Humans have been building in the areas where they live, which forces the animals to move. Dogs are especially dangerous to armadillos. Armadillos aren't very pretty, but we need to protect them if we can.

13 Why can't most armadillos roll themselves into balls?

   A Their claws are too strong.

   B Their legs are too long.

   C Their shells are made of bone.

   D They have too much fat.

14 What does the armadillo do well?

   F dig for food

   G roll into a ball

   H hide from other animals

   J swim

15 Which of the following is the armadillo most likely to eat?

   A stones

   B sand

   C rotting tree bark

   D a dead squirrel

16 Dogs are dangerous to armadillos. Dogs can _____ and injure or kill them.

   F lick

   G bark

   H ignore

   J attack

17 Why are armadillos in danger?

   A The world is getting warmer.

   B People and dogs are harming them.

   C Insects are becoming easier to find.

   D They are getting new diseases.

Here is a label from a box of cereal. Read the label. Then do Numbers 18 through 21.

Nutrition Facts

Serving Size 1 Cup
Servings Per Container About 12

Amount Per Serving	Cereal	Cereal with 1/2 Cup Milk
Calories	110	150
	% daily value	
Total Fat 0g	0%	0%
Saturated Fat 0g	0%	0%
Trans Fat 0g	0%	0%
Cholesterol 0mg	0%	0%
Sodium 220mg	9%	11%
Potassium 35mg	1%	7%
Total Carbohydrate 25g	8%	10%
Dietary Fiber less than 1g		
Sugars 3g		
Other Carbohydrates 21g		
Protein 2g		

18 What is listed before "Total Fat" on this label?

F Calories

G Cholesterol

H Sodium

J Protein

19 How many calories are in one serving of this cereal without milk?

A 25

B 40

C 110

D 150

20 What percentage of daily sodium does one serving of this cereal with milk have?

F 0 percent

G 8 percent

H 11 percent

J 100 percent

21 Which of these is not found on the label?

A Serving Size

B Amount Per Serving

C Dietary Fiber

D Size of Bowl

This is a dictionary entry for the word *bank*. Study the entry. Then do Numbers 22 through 25.

> **bank** (bank) *noun* **1.** a mound, pile, or ridge that rises above surrounding land **2.** a business that deals in money **3.** a place where things are collected and stored **4.** a group of objects arranged in a row

22 "Turn left and head to the bank of elevators." Which definition of the word *bank* is used in this sentence?

F definition 1

G definition 2

H definition 3

J definition 4

23 "I cashed the check yesterday at my bank." Which definition of the word *bank* is used in this sentence?

A definition 1

B definition 2

C definition 3

D definition 4

24 "The river bank kept the flood waters from reaching our backyard." Which definition of the word *bank* is used in this sentence?

F definition 1

G definition 2

H definition 3

J definition 4

25 "Donated blood is stored at the blood bank until it is needed." Which definition of the word *bank* is used in this sentence?

A definition 1

B definition 2

C definition 3

D definition 4

Here is a street map. Study the map. Then do Numbers 26 through 29.

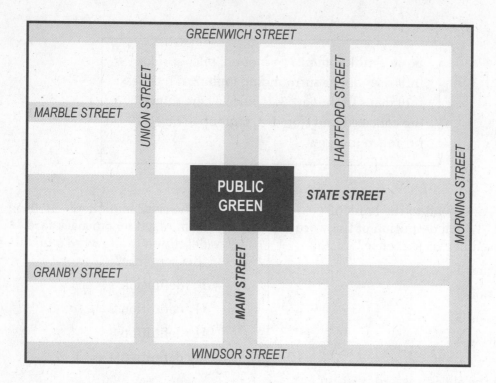

26 Which streets lead directly to the Public Green?

F   Union Street and Granby Street

G   Marble Street and Hartford Street

H   Main Street and State Street

J   Morning Street and Windsor Street

27 Which street ends at Greenwich Street?

A   Union Street

B   State Street

C   Granby Street

D   Marble Street

28 What is in the center of the town?

F   Granby Street

G   Morning Street

H   a house

J   Public Green

29 Which street is the farthest from Greenwich Street?

A   State Street

B   Windsor Street

C   Granby Street

D   Marble Street

Study this bill. Then do Numbers 30 through 33.

ABC Gas & Electric Co.
P. O. Box 4321
Boston, MA 02118

Account # 1213

Amount Due   **$213.71**
Bill Date   07/28/09
Due Date   08/17/09

Amount Enclosed

$ [,   .]

Make check payable to:
ABC Gas & Electric Co.
P. O. Box 4321
Boston, MA 02118

Anna B. Jones
956 Main Street
North Andover, MA 01845

30 This is a bill for which company?

F   Anna B. Jones

G   The Jones Co.

H   ABC Gas & Electric Co.

J   Boston, MA

31 What is the total amount owed for this bill?

A $213.71

B $24.17

C $1,234.56

D $21.71

32 When must this bill be paid?

F   January 8, 2009

G   August 17, 2009

H   July 28, 2009

J   December 14, 2009

33 To what address should this bill and payment be mailed?

A   P.O. Box 7777
    North Andover, MA 01845

B   956 Main Street
    North Andover, MA 01845

C   P.O. Box 4321
    Boston, MA 02118

D   956 Main Street
    Boston, MA 02118

Page 71

Go On ▶

This passage is about President Roosevelt. Read the passage. Then do Numbers 34 and 35.

Have you ever been to a national park? If you have, thank Theodore Roosevelt. "Teddy" Roosevelt was the twenty-sixth president. He was 42 when he took office in 1901. He is still the youngest person to have held the job. It was Roosevelt who signed a law creating the first five national parks.

Roosevelt was a man of great energy. He was weak and often sick as a boy, but he had a strong will. He overcame poor health with exercise and fresh air. He believed deeply in staying active. He ranched in the West for awhile. He started an army troop called the Rough Riders. They became famous in a war against Spain. He traveled around the world. He wrote more than 35 books. He also wrote thousands and thousands of letters in his life. He also was known for starting the Panama Canal and winning the Nobel Peace Prize. But Roosevelt was probably best known for trying to help save our country's land and animals.

34 Which word best describes Theodore Roosevelt?
F angry
G active
H greedy
J lazy

35 What effect did Roosevelt's boyhood have on him?
A He stayed ill for much of his life.
B He avoided struggle.
C He believed in the benefits of exercise and activity.
D He became the youngest president.

This passage is about President Roosevelt's influence on the National Parks System. Read the passage. Then do Numbers 36 through 41.

In the early years of the twentieth century, wild places in the United States were disappearing. The nation was growing. Some Americans were troubled by the disappearing wild spaces. Others only wanted to make money from the land. President Roosevelt loved nature and animals and didn't want to see them disappear. He realized that national parks could draw people and create business for the state and federal governments. Presidents had the power to protect the land, but few had done so.

Roosevelt took action. He created the National Park System, but he still wasn't satisfied. He used his presidential powers to create 150 national forests. He also created the first 18 national monuments, 51 bird reservations, and 4 national game preserves. Today the National Park System includes almost 400 protected areas. Thanks to President Roosevelt, Americans can enjoy nature in almost every U.S. state.

36 Why did Roosevelt create the National Parks System?

   F He wanted to be elected again.

   G He knew the parks would make money.

   H He was forced to by the law.

   J He loved nature and animals.

37 Which statement is the main idea of this passage?

   A Today there are almost 400 national parks.

   B Wild spaces are disappearing in the United States.

   C Theodore Roosevelt was a man of action.

   D Theodore Roosevelt played a huge role in creating national parks.

38 According to the passage, what effect did the nation's growth have on the country?

   F Fewer people moved to the West.

   G It led to a war with Spain.

   H Wild spaces began to disappear.

   J Many people voted for Roosevelt.

39 How did creating parks change land use?

   A To this point, little land had been protected.

   B Parks could no longer draw people and make money.

   C The parks slowed the growth of the nation.

   D Park areas were now open for any purpose.

40 How did Roosevelt differ from presidents who came before him?

   F He was easily elected.

   G He acted to protect the land.

   H He fought for what he believed was right.

   J He was not elected again.

41 Why was Roosevelt able to create so many protected areas?

   A Most people agreed with him.

   B He had the power of his office.

   C Few people paid attention to him.

   D He cared about the outdoors.

This passage is about keeping your car in good shape. Read the passage. Then do Numbers 42 through 45.

Owning a car is not just about driving around. A car needs to be cared for so that it will last you a long time. You can keep your car in good shape by following some simple rules.

First, you should make sure that your car is filled with the right fluids. Your car will let you know when it is low on gas, but you should also check the fluids for other parts of the car, like the windshield wipers and brakes. If any of these fluids are low, you can replace them yourself or take the car to a mechanic.

Second, make sure to get your car's oil changed every three months. This will help the car's engine run better. When you take your car in, the mechanic will also check the tire pressure and other parts to make sure everything looks good.

Lastly, get a tune up for your car every 30,000 miles. This is like taking your car in for a check-up. Whoever works on your car will check the spark plugs, muffler, battery, and engine, and replace anything that is not working right.

Follow these rules, and you will have your car for a long time!

42 The main idea of this passage is

   F to explain how to change the tire on a car

   G to explain how to drive a car

   H to explain how to keep your car running smoothly

   J to explain how a tune up works

43 What conclusion can you draw from this passage?

   A Keeping your car running smoothly is possible.

   B Keeping your car running smoothly is impossible.

   C You need lots of tools to keep your car running smoothly.

   D You need to take a class to learn how to keep your car running smoothly.

44 Which of the following is a fact?

   F Refilling windshield wiper fluid is difficult.

   G Mechanics are better than drivers at changing the oil.

   H Checking the fluid levels is easy to do.

   J Cars show you when the tank of gas is empty.

45 If you follow the instructions in this passage, you can predict that

   A an oil change will cost you a lot of money

   B your car will last a long time

   C replacing fluids will take a long time

   D you will need help from a mechanic to fill your gas tank

This passage is about a veterinarian. Read the passage. Then do Numbers 46 through 50.

My veterinarian, Dr. Wiseman, is the best I have ever known. She is a great doctor, and she is fun to talk to. She is always fair and honest. Unlike some other vets, she always gives me a cost estimate and asks for my OK before doing any work on my cat.

Last week, for example, I dropped off my cat at the animal hospital for a teeth cleaning. Dr. Wiseman called me and said that she noticed two of Samantha's teeth were developing cavities. She said she could pull both teeth while she had Samantha at the clinic. I told Dr. Wiseman the cost of pulling the teeth would break my budget for the month. I asked whether I could put off having the teeth pulled for a short time. Would it be dangerous for Samantha? No, Dr. Wiseman said, it could wait a few weeks if needed.

Dr. Wiseman helps me keep my cat and my budget in good shape. Plus, she's really nice, too!

46 What is the main idea of the passage?

F The writer decides not to have Samantha's teeth pulled.

G The writer thinks that her veterinarian is the best.

H The writer takes her cat in for a teeth cleaning.

J Dr. Wiseman is honest.

47 Which statement accurately describes Dr. Wiseman?

A She is always fair and honest.

B She does extra tests without asking if it's OK.

C She is a bad doctor.

D She doesn't like animals.

48 Which statement is an opinion?

F Dr. Wiseman helps keep my cat healthy.

G Last week I dropped my cat off for a teeth cleaning.

H Dr. Wiseman works at a local animal clinic.

J My veterinarian is the best veterinarian ever.

49 My vet has always been honest with me. I _____ her.

A trust

B dislike

C fear

D amuse

50 Which statement is a fact?

F Dr. Wiseman is a veterinarian.

G Dr. Wiseman is a great veterinarian.

H Dr. Wiseman is fun to talk to.

J Dr. Wiseman is a really nice person.

Page 75

STOP

Lesson 1 Practice (page 7)

1. **C** The directory is arranged in alphabetical order by name. Office numbers follow the names and are not in order (option A). Floors and types of businesses (options B and D) are in no particular order.

2. **G** Hall Eyewear is in Office 124 and would be the place to get glasses. No other office would offer this service.

3. **B** Dr. Nelson's office is Office 128. The other options are not doctor's offices.

4. **G** Paintbrushes would most likely be kept near paint. Paintbrushes would not be found with Lawn & Garden equipment (option F), Door Hardware (option H), or Kitchen Appliances (option J).

5. **C** Door handles would most likely be sold in Door Hardware, not in Lawn & Garden (option A), Paint & Wallpaper (option B), or Kitchen Appliances (option D).

Lesson 2 Practice (page 9)

1. **C** If you enter from the South Gate, the baseball field is on the left. Option B, the rose garden, is on the right. The other options are on the opposite side of the park.

2. **J** If you enter the park through the North Gate, you'll walk between the picnic area and the playground. The other options surround different entrances to the park.

3. **D** If you enter the park through the West Gate, you will walk between the picnic area and baseball field. The other options surround different entrances to the park.

4. **F** The rose garden is between the South and East gates. The baseball field is between the South and West gates (option G). The picnic area is between the West and North gates (option H). The playground is between the North and East gates (option J).

Lesson 3 Practice (page 11)

1. **C** The title of the graph and the key show that the graph is about the number of employees that work for the shipping company. The graph provides no information about trucks (option A) or money (option B). The graph shows the number of employees, not the number of people who applied for jobs (option D).

2. **G** The graph shows that 10 people work in the office. There are 5 employees (option F) in labeling and 30 employees (option J) in shipping. No bar on the graph shows 20 employees (option H).

3. **B** Packing and transport both have 15 employees; the bars for these two groups are the same length. The

other options are incorrect because none of the other bars on the graph shows the same number of employees; the other bars are all different lengths.

4. **F** Shipping has the most employees; it has the longest bar on the graph. The other options are incorrect because they all have bars that are shorter than shipping, which means they have fewer employees.

Lesson 4 Practice (page 13)

1. **C** The FIRST AID section tells where to call for help if the product is swallowed. The label does not tell how to use the product (option A), fire safety tips (option B), or what the product is made of (option D).

2. **G** The label says the cleaner may be harmful or fatal if swallowed and may burn eyes and skin, so option G is correct. The label does not contain any information about the other options.

3. **A** Fifteen minutes is the correct answer. The other options are incorrect according to the instructions in the FIRST AID section of the label.

4. **F** The label says to "get immediate help from a doctor," so option F is correct. The label does not mention calling a lawyer (option G), the police (option H), or the fire department (option J).

5. **C** The WARNING section of the label says the product is "harmful or fatal if swallowed." The label does not mention the product being safe for everyone (option A), wearing a mask (option B), or animals (option D).

Lesson 5 Practice (page 15)

1. **A** Both the direction line and the information in the form talk about getting cash back. Options B, C, and D, are incorrect because this information is not mentioned on the form.

2. **H** The limit is 8 quarts or $8.00. The other options are incorrect because the form states that there is a limit of 8 quarts.

3. **D** The form states that offer is only valid for purchases made up to January 31, 2010. Option A is the first date of purchase the rebate applies to, not the last. Option B is well after the dates the rebate applies to. Option C is well before the dates the rebate applies to.

4. **H** To get the rebate, you need the completed form and the original sales receipt. Other options are incorrect because the form says nothing about a label (option F), canceled check (option G), or a bar code (option J).

1. **B** Insurance benefits are an example of definition 2. The other options do not apply to insurance payments.

2. **F** Good eating habits can make your health, and your life, better. The other options give other meanings of the word.

3. **C** This sentence uses *benefit* to describe an event that will help others (definition 3). The other options give different meanings of the word.

4. **H** The city should no longer be affected by unpleasant pollution (definition 3). The other options give other meanings of the word.

5. **D** The speaker notes that he or she is busy in the morning, but free, or not busy, in the afternoon. The other options give other meanings of the word.

TABE Review: Interpret Graphic Information (pages 18–21)

1. **D** This sign is for a sale on shoes. Options A, B, and C are incorrect because these items are not listed on the sign. [Signs]

2. **G** Shoes marked with a red tag are $5 off. Options F and H are incorrect because items with yellow tags are $10 off. Option J is incorrect because not all items are $5 off. [Signs]

3. **B** The sentence is saying that Mr. Sandoval would be capable of being in charge of the day-to-day operations of the company. The other options give different meanings of the word. [Dictionary Usage]

4. **H** The speaker is going to try to get elected as treasurer of the neighborhood association (definition 3). The other options give different meanings of the word. [Dictionary Usage]

5. **D** The bar is longest for Texas, which means it has the most tornadoes. All other options are incorrect because their bars are shorter than the bar for Texas, which means they have fewer tornadoes. [Graphs]

6. **F** The bar is shortest for Nebraska, which means it has the fewest tornadoes. All other options are incorrect because their bars are longer than the bar for Nebraska, which means they have more tornadoes. [Graphs]

7. **B** The bar almost reaches the halfway point between 40 and 60. Option A is incorrect because the bar goes past the line for 40. Options C and D are incorrect because the bar does not reach either the lines for 60 or 80, so the number must be lower. [Graphs]

8. **G** The bar for Texas is more than twice as long as any other bar, which means it has more than twice as many tornadoes. Option F is incorrect because the bar for Oklahoma is shorter than the one for Florida. Option H is incorrect because the bar for Nebraska goes well beyond the line for 20 tornadoes. Option J is incorrect because the bar for Florida does not get close to the line for 100 tornadoes. [Graphs]

9. **B** The correct answer is 13. This is the number next to the picture of a clock and above the message, "for wake-up calls." Option A is not listed as an option on the phone. Option C is the number for voice mail. Option D is the number for room service. [Consumer Materials]

10. **H** The correct answer is 14. This is the number next to the picture of a mailbox and above the message, "for voice mail." Option F is not listed as an option on the phone. Option G is the number for wake-up calls. Option J is the number for room service. [Consumer Materials]

11. **A** The form requires the patient to fill in his or her name. Option B is incorrect because the form provides the doctors' names; it does not request this information. Options C and D are incorrect because this information is not mentioned on the form. [Forms]

12. **H** The form tells patients to "expect to wait approximately 15 minutes." The wait time does not depend on the appointment or check-in times (options F and G). Option J is incorrect because the form says 15 minutes, not 30 minutes. [Forms]

13. **D** The police department is on the corner of Second Avenue and Morgan Street. Options A, B, and C are incorrect because these places are all on Wilson Street. [Maps]

14. **H** The library is right across the street from the school. All of the other buildings are farther away from the school. [Maps]

15. **C** The school is on the corner of First Avenue and Wilson Street. Option A is incorrect because the school is not on Morgan Street. Option B is incorrect because the school is not on Second Avenue. Option D is incorrect because the school is not on Morgan Street or Second Avenue. [Maps]

16. **H** The bank is right across the street from the park. All of the other options are farther away from the park. [Maps]

Lesson 7 Practice (page 23)

1. **C** *Clogged* and *blocked* mean about the same thing: that something is so full nothing can get through. Streets that are completely full of cars, trucks, and buses would not be open (option A), safe (option B), or beautiful (option D).

2. **F** The word *block* in the second sentence gives the reader a clue about the meaning of *clogged*. The other options do not help the reader understand *clogged*.

3. **D** If something makes you miss appointments or be late for work, it causes problems, or trouble for you. It would not be funny (option A) or easy (option C). Though traffic can be dangerous (option B), this meaning is not related to the rest of the sentence.

4. **G** If something eases, it becomes lighter in degree, quantity, or intensity. Recording (option F), studying (option H), and ignoring (option J) the problem of overcrowding will not make the problem go away.

1. B *Scattered* means "spread across a wide area." The opposite of this is *gathered.* Options A and D have meanings that are similar to *scattered.* Option C is not related to the meaning of *scattered.*

2. J *Ideal* means "perfect." The opposite of this is *awful.* Options F and G mean the same thing as *ideal.* Option H means neither ideal nor awful. It means "just good enough."

3. A *Thunderous* means "loud and booming." The opposite of this is *quiet.* Options B and C mean the same thing as *thunderous.* Option D is not related to the meaning of *thunderous.*

4. G *Festive* means "joyful and celebratory." The opposite of this is *serious.* Options F and H mean the same thing as *festive.* Option J is not related to the meaning of *festive.*

1. B The word *cry* indicates the appropriate word is *sad.* The other options do not make sense in the context of crying.

2. F The word *layoffs* indicates the appropriate word is *nervous;* Carin is worried she might lose her job. The other options do not make sense in the context of layoffs.

3. C The word *wash* indicates the appropriate word is *dry.* It does not make sense to wash and use the dishes (option A), wash and hide the dishes (option B), or wash and break the dishes (option D).

4. H The word *library* indicates the appropriate word is *book.* The other options do not relate to a library.

5. D The phrase *save up for a long time* indicates that the car Joelle wanted was expensive. The other options do not make sense in the context of having to save for a long time.

6. F The words *picnic* and *trees* indicate that the appropriate word is *park.* The other options do not make sense in the context of picnics and trees.

7. D *Watch* is the most appropriate word in the context of knowing what time it is. The other options do not relate to this context.

8. H The word *tropical* indicates that *beach* is the most appropriate word. The other options do not relate to the context of a tropical vacation.

1. B *Unlucky* means the opposite of *fortunate.* The phrase *you may not be* so *lucky* gives the clue. Option A means the same thing as *fortunate.* Options C and D are not related to the meaning of *fortunate.* [Opposite Meaning]

2. F *Ordinary* and *common* mean about the same thing. Options G and H mean the opposite of *common.* Option J does not relate to the meaning of *common.* [Same Meaning]

3. D *More* means "a greater number." This is the opposite of *fewer.* Options A and B have meanings that are similar to *fewer.* Option C means "bigger in size" rather than "a greater number." [Opposite Meaning]

4. J *Totally* and *completely* mean about the same thing. Option F means the opposite of *completely.* Options G and H are not related to the meaning of *completely.* [Same Meaning]

5. C The passage says that unless humans change their behaviors, more types of frogs are doomed to die out. This means they are certain to die out. Options A and B mean the opposite of *doomed.* Option D only means there is a chance the frogs will die out, not that it is bound to happen. [Same Meaning]

6. H *Small* means about the same thing as *minor* in this context. The clue is the phrase *large or minor.* Options F and G mean the opposite of *minor.* If something is noticeable (option J), it is likely to be large, not small or minor. [Same Meaning]

7. A *Necessary* and *needed* mean about the same thing. If something is necessary, it is needed. Options B and C mean the opposite of *necessary.* While something that is necessary may also be helpful (option D), these two words do not mean the same thing. [Same Meaning]

8. F If you waste money, you do not save it. These two words have opposite meanings. Options G and H have similar meanings to *waste.* Option J is not related to the meaning of *waste.* [Opposite Meaning]

9. B Your main goals are your most important goals. They are the goals you focus on first. Options A and C mean the opposite of *main.* Option D does not directly relate to the meaning of *main.* [Same Meaning]

10 J If someone is squinting in the sun, they must have forgotten their sunglasses. The other options would not help keep the sun out of someone's eyes. [Appropriate Word]

11. B The word *boss* indicates the correct answer is *meeting.* Joaquin's boss would probably not care if he were late to a doctor's appointment (option A), dinner (option C), or a movie (option D). [Appropriate Word]

12. H The words *letter* and *desk* indicate the correct answer is *stamp.* You need a stamp to mail a letter, and you might fight a stamp in your desk. You do not need a ruler to mail a letter (option F), and you would not likely find a mailman (option G) or a post office (option J) in your desk. [Appropriate Word]

13. A You would put dirty clothes into a washing machine. It does not make sense to put clean (option B), new (option C), or folded clothes (option D) into a washing machine. [Appropriate Word]

14. G The words *calling* and *ringing* indicate the correct answer is cell *phone.* While the other options may make noise, you would not receive a call on them. [Appropriate Word]

15. B The words *crib* and *nursery* indicate the correct answer is *baby.* The other options do not make sense in the context of a crib and new nursery. [Appropriate Word]

16. F The word *feet* indicates the correct answer is *shoes.* The other answers do not make sense in the context of someone's feet hurting. [Appropriate Word]

17. A The word *fruit* indicates the correct answer is *apples.* The other options do not make sense in the context of fruit. [Appropriate Word]

Lesson 10 Practice (page 32)

1. C The passage says that the two most-collected tractors are John Deere and International Farmall. Options A, B, and D are other brands mentioned in the passage, but no mention is made about them being the most collected.

2. J International Farmalls are bright red. The colors of options F and G are not stated in the passage. John Deere tractors (option H) are green.

3. C John Deere tractors are known as "Johnny Poppers." This name is not used to describe any of the other tractors. The other options are not associated with this name.

4. J The passage states that the great age of American farm tractors lasted from about 1950 to 1970. Options F, G, and H are not mentioned.

Lesson 11 Practice (page 34)

1. C According to step 1, right after choosing a shady spot, you check to make sure all doors and windows are closed. Drying the car (option A), filling a bucket with water (option B), and washing the car with a soapy sponge or cloth (option D) all come after the first step in the list.

2. G In step 4, washing one side of the car with a soapy sponge or cloth happens right before spraying the soap suds off. Drying the car (option F), the final rinse (option H), and repeating the steps (option J) all happen after step 4.

3. D The list tells you to use a hose to spray off the dirt in Step 3, right after you fill a bucket with water in step 2, which means it couldn't happen before that (option A). Washing one side of the car (option B) is incorrect because it happens in step 4. Choosing a shady spot (option C) happens first.

4. F In step 6, drying the car with a towel happens after the final rinse in step 5. Options G, H, and J happen before step 6.

Lesson 12 Practice (page 36)

1. C Readers like photos, so the newspapers add them to articles. Option A is incorrect because photos are not related to ads. Adding photos (option B) doesn't cut costs. Newspapers want more readers, not less (option D).

2. J The cost of an ad is based on its size and how many readers will see the ad. Options F, G, and H are

incorrect because they have nothing to do with the cost of an ad.

3. C The passage states that businesses want to place their ads in the sections that most people read. Local news and lifestyle are the most popular sections, so option D is incorrect. The passage does not mention whether businesses like world news (option A) or the costs of advertising in this section (option B).

4. H The local and lifestyle sections are larger sections. The passage doesn't mention how large the sports highlights are (option F). The national and world news sections (option G) are smaller. The classifieds (option J) do not appear in the passage.

TABE Review: Recall Information (pages 37–39)

1. D The second sentence explains that electric cars have been around since the 1900s. Option A is incorrect because electric were not invented until after the 1800s. Options B and C are incorrect because these details are not mentioned in the passage. [Details]

2. H The first electric cars couldn't go very far. Option F is incorrect because being quiet is not a problem. Option G is incorrect because the passage doesn't state that they cost too much. Option J is incorrect because the passage doesn't discuss the number of electric car parts. [Details]

3. B The passage states that first gas-powered cars were hard to start. The passage states that cars that ran on gas were noisy, so option F is incorrect. The passage states that electric cars, not gas-powered cars, were unable to travel far, so option H is incorrect. The passage does not say that the cars needed new parts, so option D is incorrect. [Details]

4. J The first sentence states that electric cars are not a new idea. Option F is incorrect because the cars were popular in the past. Option G is incorrect because the passage does not mention how much energy electric cars use. Option H is incorrect because the passage does not discuss how easy or difficult the cars were to drive. [Stated Concepts]

5. C Lincoln became president in early 1861, before the Battle of Gettysburg. Options A, B, and D are incorrect because these events all took place after the Battle of Gettysburg. [Sequence]

6. F The South won several battles and looked as if it might win the war. Option G is incorrect because Lincoln called for more troops after the South looked like it might win the war. Option H is incorrect because Lee surrendered to Grant at the very end of the war. Option J is incorrect because the North began to win more battles after the South's early wins. [Sequence]

7. D Lee surrendered to Grant in April 1865. The events listed in the other options took place before 1865. [Details]

8. H The South did well early in the war, but the North's strength showed itself when they won the war. Option F is incorrect because the North did not win quickly. Option G is incorrect because the South had fewer more men and arms. Option J is incorrect because the South did not win. [Stated Concepts]

9. **B** Most companies use trucks to get things to market. Options A, C, and D are incorrect because the passage says clearly that trucks are the most used form of transport. [Stated Concept]

10. **H** About eighty percent of all U.S. shipping goes by truck. Options F, G, and J are incorrect because these figures do not appear in the passage. [Details]

11. **D** Trains carry loads more cheaply than trucks. Option A is incorrect because trains cannot go door to door. Options B and C are incorrect because the passage does not discuss the speed of trains or the fuel they use. [Stated Concept]

12. **J** Higher fuel prices are problematic for the trucking business. The other options did not appear in the passage. [Details]

Lesson 13 Practice (page 41)

1. **A** The comparison of Matisse to a wild beast plunging at something it loves indicates that he threw himself into his art out of love. Options B, C, and D are incorrect because they don't make sense with the information from the passage.

2. **H** You can tell Henri was determined because he didn't give up after people laughed at him. Nothing in the passage indicates he was angry (option F), weak (option G), or shy (option J).

Lesson 14 Practice (page 43)

1. **A** The passage says that Americans fell in love with their cars and that more families owned cars, so it was a good time for Americans and their cars. Option B is true, but it is a detail, not the main idea. Options C and D are incorrect because they are not mentioned in the passage.

2. **H** The passage shows the many different ways cars had changed. The passage does not talk about how fast cars were, so option F is wrong. Options G (soft seats) and J (shiny bumpers) are incorrect because they are simply about the many changes cars had gone through.

Lesson 15 Practice (Page 45)

1. **B** Joan dug up a spot in her yard because she decided to plant a garden. Option A is incorrect because it is a detail about planting a garden. Options C and D are incorrect because they are not mentioned in the passage.

2. **F** The passage says that the plants were growing and healthy. The passage does not mention Joan actually eating the vegetables (option G); it says she was looking forward to eating them. The passage does not mention heavy rains (option H) or Joan starting a farmer's market (option J).

Lesson 16 Practice (Page 47)

1. **A** When you contrast the numbers, you see there are 6 students in the Sculpture class and 4 students in the Paint class. This means there are more students in Sculpture than in Paint. There are more students in Coal than in Sculpture (option B). There are the same number of students in Chalk as Sculpture (option C). Ink is not listed as a class (option D).

2. **J** When you compare and contrast the numbers, you see that there are more students in Coal than in any other class. Options F and G are incorrect because fewer students take Paint than Sculpture or Chalk. Option H is incorrect because there are the same number of students in Sculpture and Chalk.

3. **C** Both mowers have sharp blades. Options A and B only apply to gas-powered mowers. Option D only applies to manual mowers.

4. **J** When you compare the times, you find that Stretching and Jogging are both 10 minutes. Options F, G, and H are not correct because these exercises all have varying times.

Lesson 17 Practice (Page 49)

1. **B** The backyard is best suited for a golden retriever. The passage says golden retrievers are calm dogs and do not need a lot of space to play. Since Anna's backyard is small, you can conclude the backyard is better for golden retrievers. Border collies (option A) are lively and need room to run, so Anna's backyard would be too small. Biking (option C) and swimming (option D) are activities they do at the park, not in their backyard.

2. **H** Anna and her family are very active—they bike, swim, and hike, so you can conclude they enjoy outdoor activities. Option F is incorrect because they ride bikes, swim, and hike, which are all forms of exercise. Option G is incorrect because they are buying a dog, which means they like animals. Option J is incorrect because the family has a small yard.

3. **C** Therin is most likely at a park—she walks her dog, she can hear birds, and she can see the sun, which are things that a person does outside. Therin would not be able to do these things in a supermarket (option A), at a movie (option B), or on a plane (option D).

4. **F** The ad does not mention the time when the class begins, so a person would check the Web site for this information. A person would not check the Web site for information that is already listed in the ad. The ad tells that the class is at Zilker Part (option G), that is on Thursdays (option H), and that all dogs are welcome (option J).

TABE Review: Construct Meaning (pages 50–53)

1. **C** The passage is all about volleyball player Gabrielle Reece. Option A is incorrect because the passage is about a specific person, not multiple people. While the passage mentions college volleyball (option B), this is only a detail. Option D is incorrect because

the passage does not teach how to play volleyball. [Main Idea]

2. H Turning down jobs to finish her education means that Gabrielle valued school. Options F and J are incorrect because the passage doesn't say if she didn't like work or if she was shy. Option G is incorrect because finishing school doesn't mean that she wanted to play in the Olympics. [Character Aspects]

3. A Eating a variety of fruits and vegetables will ensure you get a variety of nutrients. Option B is incorrect because this will decrease your risk of disease. Option C is incorrect because fats, sugars, and salts impact your health in a negative way. Option D is incorrect because the passage does not indicate that eating fruits and vegetables will help you remember anything. [Cause and Effect]

4. G The first paragraph states that businesses advertise so that you will buy their products. While some business may want you to be healthy (option F) and live longer (option H), this is not a directly stated cause-and-effect relationship found in the passage. There is no information in the passage to suggest that businesses want you to start your own business (option J). [Cause and Effect]

5. C Andrew promised to only use his phone for important things, but he didn't. This caused problems that made his parents upset. Staying out late (option A) and not paying his bill (option B) are incorrect because they aren't mentioned in the passage. Option D is incorrect because his parents wanted him to call home. [Cause and Effect]

6. J Texting in class makes the teacher angry. Nothing is said about a bad grade (Option F), homework (Option G), or answering the cell phone in class (Option H). [Cause and Effect]

7. A The passage is about how Andrew uses his cell phone. At first he was doing well; then he had problems. Option B is incorrect because the passage doesn't say that he loves his phone. Options C and D are incorrect because they are details that support the main idea. [Main Idea]

8. H Andrew's talking on the phone too much means that he likes talking on the phone. The passage does not say that Andrew has problems with the law (option F). The passage doesn't say what kind of student Andrew is (option G). Andrew does not always keep his promises; for example, he had promised to only use his phone for very important things, but then he started talking on his phone too much. (option J). [Character Aspects]

9. C Andrew's parents warned him about using his minutes and he used more than he had, so the bill is likely going to be expensive. There is nothing in the passage to suggest that his phone bill is in the mail box (option A), unpaid (option B), or late (option D). [Conclusions]

10. G 15 cookbooks were sold in July, and 10 were sold in April. This means more cookbooks were sold in July than in April. Option F is incorrect because March

had the same sales as July. Options H and J are incorrect because May and June had more sales than July. [Compare and Contrast]

11. D March and July both had sales of 15 cookbooks. Option A is incorrect because April had fewer sales than July. Option B is incorrect because May had the most sales. Option C is incorrect because more cookbooks were sold in March than in April. [Compare and Contrast]

12. G Tessa is working on the computer, talking to a customer, and waving to a co-worker. Based on this information, you can conclude that she is working in an office. Option F is incorrect because she is not studying and she talks on the phone—you should not talk on a phone in a library. Tessa is waving to a co-worker, not directing traffic (option H). Tessa is writing an e-mail, not a symphony (option J). [Conclusions]

13. A The flyer is all about yoga classes for expectant moms—the classes are called Mommy-to-Be classes, and the flyer says that classes are for expectant moms. The flyer mentions beginning poses (option B), relaxation (option C), and the yoga studio (option D), but those are all details of the main idea. [Main Idea]

14. G The flyer does not say where the studio is located, so you can conclude that a person would call to get the location. The other options are listed on the flyer. The flyer says that classes begin at 1:00 and 5:00 (option F). The flyer also says that the classes are everyday (option H) and that the classes are for expectant mothers (option J). [Conclusions]

15. C The passage says that beavers and muskrats are excellent swimmers. It also states the muskrats eat fish and that beavers build dams. You can conclude the beavers and muskrats need to be near water and trees, so a river near a forest is the best-suited environment. A dry desert (option A) would not be appropriate because both animals need water and trees, two things that are not in the desert. Neither animals like humans, so a ship (option B) and a residential neighborhood (option D) would not be appropriate. Option B is also incorrect because beavers and muskrats need to be in the water, not sailing on top of it. [Conclusions]

16. J The passage states that both animals are rodents. Options F and G are only about beavers. Option H is only about muskrats. [Compare and Contrast]

17. B The passage states the Lincoln did not want the country to be divided, which shows that he loved his country. Nothing in the passage indicates that he was mean and selfish (option A) or that he was a great writer (option C). While the passage says that he was willing to fight for his country, it does not say that he pushed people around (option D). [Character Aspects]

18. H When you compare the times, you see that green beans and squash can both be introduced when a baby is 7–8 months old. The other options all have different times. [Compare and Contrast]

1. D The statement about the volcano being an amazing sight in the rain is an opinion. Some people may not think this sight is amazing. The other options are facts, not opinions.

2. G The article says Mauna Kea is the tallest mountain. The map proves this information. Options F, H, and J are all opinions. Some people might not agree with these statements, and they cannot be proven.

1. D The passage states that Daria was unhappy with the quality of photos from her regular digital camera and that the film camera took incredible photos. It also states that she wanted to take great pictures at her daughter's birthday, and that a store down the street offered lessons about how to use the film camera. From this information, we can predict that Daria will take the lessons to learn how to use the old film camera. Option A is not related to the information in the passage. Based on the information in the passage, Daria would not likely pack away the old camera (option B); she would use it. Similarly, she would not likely buy a new digital camera (option C) if she was not satisfied with the quality of digital photos.

2. H Based on the information in the passage, it makes sense that Daria would learn how to use the film camera and the two lenses that came with it. It is not likely that Daria would get rid of the two expensive lenses or pack them away (options F, G, and J).

3. A The passage states that the film camera took better photos than Daria's regular digital camera, and that Daria wanted to take great photos of her daughter's birthday. It makes sense that she would use the film camera to take photos that day. Since Daria has not been satisfied with the quality of her digital pictures, options B and C are not likely outcomes. Option D is not supported by any information in the passage.

1. D It can be proven that the United States holds elections each year. Option A is an opinion; some people may not agree that it is important to vote. Option B is an opinion. Some people think that their votes don't matter. Others disagree. Option C is also an opinion. People often disagree on the qualifications of those running for election. [Fact/Opinion]

2. G Some people think voting is very important. This is an opinion because some people believe that voting is not important. Option F is a fact. Election Day is the first Tuesday of November. Option H is a fact about voting. The results of elections are decided by the voters. Option J is a fact. It can be proven through research that there have been elections where the person won by a few votes. [Fact/Opinion]

3. C It is an opinion that the 2008 election was the most important ever. Some historians may think that other elections earlier in our country's history were more important. Option A is a fact. It can be proven that African Americans have had to struggle to win the same rights as other Americans. Options B and D are facts; they can be proven by looking at all previous U.S. presidents. [Fact/Opinion]

4. G It can be proven that Barack Obama was elected in 2008. Option F is an opinion; it cannot be proven that race has anything to do with quality as president. Option H is an opinion. In any election, there are people who vote for opposing sides; some people did not want Obama to win. Option J is an opinion; the value judgment *more than anyone else* makes this a statement with which others may disagree. [Fact/Opinion]

5. B Mr. Robinson will probably take the job because he needs the extra money. Option A is not likely because the new job will make it easier for Mr. Robinson to support his six children. Nothing says that he will look for a job at a different company (option C) or decide to stay home with the kids (option D). [Predict Outcomes]

6. F Mr. Robinson would probably use his bonus to buy food for his family since his food budget was cut by about $100 this week. There is no evidence in the passage to indicate Mr. Robinson would buy a new cell phone (option G) or a new suit (option H). Mr. Robinson would not need to buy a new water heater (option J) because according to the passage, they just had a new one installed last week. [Predict Outcomes]

7. C The passage says that Jennifer enjoys working in her own yard and has noticed that the local landscapers always seem busy, so it makes sense that she would probably mow other people's lawns to earn money. The passage does not indicate that Jennifer would do extra chores (option A) or work in a restaurant (option B). It would not make sense for her to sell her camping gear (option D) because she is trying to earn money to go camping. [Predict Outcomes]

8. H The passage indicates that there is plenty of demand for lawn services and that Jennifer is willing to do the work. The passage indicates that the local landscapers have plenty of work, so option F is not likely. Option G is incorrect; the passage indicates that Jennifer is looking for a summer job. There is nothing in the passage to indicate that her parents will give her the money she needs (option J). [Predict Outcomes]

A. A The word *set* and the phrase *get up on time in the morning* indicate the appropriate word is *alarm*. The other options do not make sense in the context of setting something to wake you up in the morning. [Appropriate Word]

B. H The words *thunder* and *lightning* and the fact that he thinks he'll have to run for the door indicate that a storm is coming and it will rain. Aaron needs something to cover him so that he won't get wet.

Options F, G, and J are not items that will keep Aaron from getting wet.

1. B The difficulty of the recipe is a matter of opinion; it cannot be proven, and other people may disagree with the idea. The other options are all facts that are stated in the recipe. [Fact/Opinion]

2. G An option is a choice. You may or may not choose to include these items; they are not required. Neither *recipe* (option F) nor *kitchen* (option H) are related to *optional*. Option J means the opposite of *optional*. [Same Meaning]

3. A The next step after cooking the macaroni is to drain the water. Options B, C, and D are later steps. [Sequence]

4. J The instructions say to turn down the heat if the pot starts to boil over. The recipe does not say to turn off the heat (option F), turn up the heat (option G), or to stir the water (option H). [Stated Concepts]

5. B The last step is to add salt and pepper to taste. Options A and D are earlier steps. Option C is not part of the recipe. [Sequence]

6. H In this context, *bound* means *likely*, and *unlikely* is the opposite of that. Options F and J are related to different meanings of *bound*. Option G is not related to *bound*. [Opposite Meaning]

7. B The bar for baseball on the bar graph stops about halfway between 20 and 30, so 25 is the correct answer. The bar for baseball goes above 20 (option A) and stops well below 40 (option C) and 50 (option D). [Graphs]

8. J Track is the least favorite sport among members of Hill Country Gym. The bar for track is shorter than any of the other bars, indicating the fewest number of members picked track as their favorite sport. The bars for baseball (option F), football (option G), and soccer (option H) are all taller than the bar for track. [Graphs]

9. C The graph indicates that 25 people picked baseball as their favorite sport, but only 15 people picked track as their favorite sport. More people like basketball than baseball (option A), more people like soccer than football (option B), and fewer people like football than basketball (option D). [Compare/Contrast]

10. G Of all the sports on the bar graph, basketball had the tallest bar. This means that more people picked basketball as their favorite sport than any other sport, indicating that basketball would have the most participants if a tournament were held. Baseball (option F), football (option H), and soccer (option J) were all less popular than basketball. [Conclusions]

11. D The information about distance (1 mile), speed, and passing other cars are all hints that the sign is a warning about work being done on a road. This is not a sign you would see indoors in an office (option A) or in a city building (option B). You would not see this sign in a park because it is about cars, not sports and play (option C). [Signs]

12. F This sign warns drivers to slow down in a work zone. Other options are incorrect because they are not supported by the information on the sign. [Signs]

13. C The passage says that armadillos have shells made of bone. Bone is hard so the shell can't be rolled into a ball. Option A is incorrect because an armadillo's claws do not keep it from rolling into a ball. Option B is incorrect because armadillos have short legs. Option D is incorrect because the passage says that armadillos don't have much fat. [Details]

14. F The passage says the armadillos are expert diggers and talks about how they use their claws to dig for food. Option G is incorrect because armadillos cannot roll themselves into balls. The passage does not talk about hiding or swimming so options H and J are incorrect. [Details]

15. D The passage states that armadillos eat dead flesh, so an armadillo is most likely to eat a dead squirrel. The other options are not included in the passage as sources of food. [Details]

16. J The words *dangerous, injure,* and *kill* indicate that *attack* is the appropriate word. A dog that licks (option F), barks at (option G), or ignores (option H) an armadillo would not be dangerous. The dog isn't dangerous until it attacks. [Appropriate Word]

17. B Human and dog activity are discussed as causes of problems for armadillos. The other options are incorrect because they are not supported by the passage. [Stated Concepts]

18. F The information for calories is before the information about total fat. Options G, H, and J are words that are shown later on the label. [Sequence]

19. C The label says that one serving of the cereal has 110 calories without milk. Option A (25) describes carbohydrates, not calories. Option B (40) is not a number found on the label. Option D (150) gives the number of calories with milk. [Consumer Materials]

20. H The column on the right shows the percentages with milk. For sodium, the correct value is 11 percent. The line for sodium shows a value in both columns, so option F is incorrect. Option G is incorrect because it shows the percentage for carbohydrates without milk. Option J is incorrect because this number doesn't appear on the label. [Consumer Materials]

21. D The size of the bowl is not found on the label. Options A, B, and C are listed on the label. [Consumer Materials]

22. J This sentence uses *bank* to describe a group of elevators. The other options give different meanings of the word. [Dictionary]

23. B This sentence uses *bank* to describe a business that deals in money. The other options give different meanings of the word. [Dictionary]

24. F This sentence uses *bank* to describe a mound of dirt that rises above the river's edge. The other options give different meanings of the word. [Dictionary]

25. C This sentence uses *bank* to describe a place where blood is collected and stored until it is needed. The other options give different meanings of the word. [Dictionary]

26. H Main Street and State Street lead directly to the Public Green. Options F, G, and J are incorrect because these streets do not lead directly to the green. [Maps]

27. A Union Street ends at Greenwich Street. The other streets do not run into Greenwich Street. [Maps]

28. J The Public Green is in the center of town. Granby Street (option F) and Morning Street (option G) are not in the center of town. The map does not show a house (option H). [Maps]

29. B Windsor Street is the farthest from Greenwich Street. The other options are between Windsor Street and Greenwich Street. [Maps]

30. H The bill is from ABC Gas & Electric Co. The name of the company and their address are on the top of the bill on the left-hand side, and the bill says to make checks payable to them. Option F is incorrect because Anna B. Jones is the person who receives the bill. Option G is wrong because there is no Jones Co. on the bill. Option J is incorrect because Boston, MA is the city and state of the mailing address of the company, not the name of the company. [Forms]

31. A $213.71 is the total amount of money that Anna B. Jones owes to the ABC Gas & Electric Co. The other options are not amounts shown on the bill. [Forms]

32. G The bill shows a due date of August 17, 2009. The dates shown in options F and J do not appear on the bill. Option H shows the date the bill was issued, not the date it is due. [Forms]

33. C Option C shows the address where the check should be mailed. Options A and D are incorrect because they are not shown on the bill. Option B is Anna Jones's address, not the payment address. [Forms]

34. G You can tell from the information in the passage that Roosevelt was an active person. Options F and H are incorrect because the passage does not talk about anger or greed. Option J is incorrect because it does not fit with other facts of Roosevelt's life as described in the passage. [Character Aspects]

35. C Roosevelt's poor health as a child led him to be a strong believer in exercise and activity. Option A is incorrect because Roosevelt overcame his poor health. Option B is incorrect because the passage shows Roosevelt did not avoid struggle. Option D is incorrect because the passage does not show a connection between Roosevelt's youth and his age as president. [Cause and Effect]

36. J Roosevelt's love of nature made him support the idea of national parks. Option F is incorrect because there is no information in the passage about Roosevelt's election. Option G is incorrect because his motive was to protect land, not make money. Option H is incorrect because he chose to create the park system. [Stated Concept]

37. D This passage is about the role of Theodore Roosevelt in creating national parks. Options A, B, and C are incorrect because they are supporting details, not the main idea. [Main Idea]

38. H The passage tells us that as the nation grew, wild spaces disappeared. Option F is incorrect because nothing is said about people moving in any direction. Option G is incorrect because the passage does not mention a war against Spain. Option J is incorrect because the passage has no information about people voting for Roosevelt. [Cause and Effect]

39. A Before Roosevelt's actions, little land had been protected. Option B is incorrect because parks could draw people and make money. Option C is incorrect because the passage says nothing about slowing the growth of the nation. Option D is incorrect because park areas were protected, not opened. [Compare/Contrast]

40. G Unlike earlier presidents, Roosevelt acted to protect vast areas. Options F and J are incorrect because the passage does not discuss election results. Option H is incorrect. The passage does not discuss other presidents' efforts to fight for what they believed was right. [Compare/Contrast]

41. B Roosevelt successfully used the power of his office of president to create the park system. Option A is incorrect because the passage does not discuss whether most people agreed with Roosevelt. Option C is incorrect because it is an unlikely conclusion that few people paid attention to a president's ideas. Option D is incorrect. Roosevelt cared for nature, but the fact that he was president and could get the job done was what allowed him to create the parks. [Conclusions]

42. H The main idea of the passage is to explain how to keep your car running smoothly. Nothing is said about changing the tire on a car (option F) or driving a car (option G). The information about a tune up (option J) is a detail, not a main idea. [Main Idea]

43. A The passage makes clear that keeping your car running smoothly is possible if you simply follow the steps discussed. Following the steps in this passage is not impossible (option B), and you don't need a lot of tools (option C). Nothing is said about a class (option D). [Conclusions]

44. J It can be proven that cars have gauges that show when the gas tank is empty. How easy or difficult it is to change windshield wiper fluid (option F), whether mechanics are better than drivers at changing flats (option G), and whether checking fluid levels is easy to do (option H) are all opinions. People may agree or disagree on these topics. [Fact and Opinion]

45. B The directions in this passage will help you safely maintain your car for a long time. There is no reason to believe that an oil change will cost a lot of money (option A), that replacing fluids will take a long time (option C), or that you will need help from a mechanic to fill your gas tank (option D). [Predict Outcomes]

46. G This statement is the main idea of the story—the writer thinks very highly of Dr. Wiseman. Options F and H are incorrect. Both are supporting details, not the main idea. Option J describes a character trait, but it is not the main idea of the story. [Main Idea]

47. A This statement describes Dr. Wiseman based on her words and actions. Options B, C, and D do not accurately describe Dr. Wiseman according to the passage. [Character Aspects]

48. J This option is the writer's opinion about Dr. Wiseman. Other people may disagree with this idea. The other options are facts, not opinions; they can be proven to be true. [Fact and Opinion]

49. A The word *honest* indicates *trust* is the appropriate word for the blank. You would not dislike (option B) or fear (option C) an honest person. Option D is not related to being honest. [Appropriate Word]

50. F This option identifies a fact that can be proven. The other options are all opinions. They cannot be proven, and other people may disagree with them. [Fact and Opinion]